FOR
WORSHIPERS
ONLY

Secrets Of The Worshiper On How
To Host The Presence Of The Lord

SHIRO MUIRURI

Scripture references are from Strong's Exhaustive Hebrew and Greek Concordance by James Strong.

Contents

ACKNOWLEDGEMENTS

I want to thank the Lord for bringing His word over my life to pass. The vision may tarry, but it will surely come to pass! I thank my pastors Prophet Raphael and Aretha Grant for believing in me and giving me a platform to exercise my gifts. Thank you for standing with me and also covering my head in the day of battle. I will forever be grateful to you. I also want to thank the people who have been there along my journey of life and helped bring this great work into fruition. Just to mention a few – James Hilton, Grace Njeri, Mary Wambui, Carol Wanjiru, Martha Wamaitha, Sister Catherine, Faith Njenga and Lucy Njeri. To the various churches and worship teams that I've served in – Giatutu PCEA, CHMI, and Eagles Chapel, thank you all for receiving me, it has been a great delight to worship Jesus together with you. Amen

DEDICATION

I dedicate this book to my biological and spiritual parents Pastor Peter and Angelica Muiruri and my spiritual mother Prophetess Ruth Mtobi. Dad, thank you for unknowingly teaching me about worship, and modeling Fatherhood not just to me but my son Vierri as well. Mom, thank you for the many years I watched you lead praise and worship until the presence of God was made manifest in our midst. To my spiritual Mother Ruth, thank you for believing in me, loving me and praying for me. By this you helped pave the way for a generation of prophetic worshipers who have found the good thing that will not be taken away from them. This is the physical manifestation of your prayers. I promise to honor you in my life by living a life poured out before the Lord all the days of my life.

Your dear,

Shiro

INTRODUCTION

I do not have many words for an introduction because most of what I want us to learn is in the book. The only thing I'd like us to focus on is Psalm 27:4 and Luke 10:42

> *"**One thing** have I desired of the Lord, **that** will I seek after; that I may dwell in the house of the Lord all the days of my life, to behold the beauty of the Lord, and to enquire in His temple."*

> "But ***one thing is needed***, and Mary has chosen that good part, which will not be taken away from her."

> All I want is His Presence!

CHAPTER ONE

What is worship?

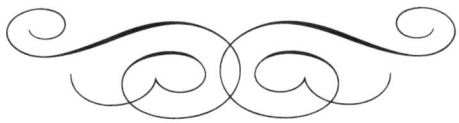

According to Meriam Webster, worship is either a verb or a noun. The verb worship is *to regard with great or extravagant respect, honor, or devotion for example, a celebrity worshipped by her fans.*

The noun worship is *extravagant respect or admiration for or devotion to an object of esteem for example, worship of the dollar.* Now let us look at the Bible references for worship in Hebrew and Greek.

Worship is when we give our entire being (spirit, soul and body) to God. The Hebrew word for worship according to Strong's concordance is *shachah* which means to depress oneself, that is, prostrate (especially reflexively in homage to royalty or God);-bow (self) down, crouch, fall down (flat), humbly beseech, do (make)) obeisance, do reverence, make to stoop.

In Greek, the word *latreuo* means to serve or to worship. Universally, to serve, minister to, either gods or men.

Proskuneo which means prostrate.

So, in our case, the WHO we are talking about worshiping here is the Almighty God. He is the object of our worship. Psalm 81:1-10 says, "*Hear, O My people, and I will admonish you! O Israel, if you will listen to Me! There shall be no foreign god among you; nor shall you worship any foreign god. I am the Lord your God, Who brought you out of the land of Egypt;*"

Deuteronomy 6:4 says, "*Hear, O Israel: The Lord our God, the Lord is one!*"

You can worship anyone or anything you like, but ONLY ONE deserves the worship. You have been given the free will to offer worship to whatever and whoever you want but remember that Only One is worthy. (removed but) Even if you choose not to worship God, you are worshiping something…or someone. Worship is not about emotionalism but about obedience. You hear people say all the time, "*oh I am not emotional*", but the same people who say this are very demonstrative in their expression of emotion during a soccer or football match. So the problem here is not emotionalism but disobedience.

Worship is first mentioned in Genesis 22:5 where it says, "*And Abraham said unto his young men, abide ye here with the ass and I and the lad will go yonder and worship and come again to you.*" This is right after the Lord asked Abraham to offer his only son, Isaac, to Him. Out of this we see that worship has nothing to do with singing. Singing is one of the expressions of worship among many others. Worship is complete obedience to the Lover of our souls where we are willing to lay our lives prostrate before Him. It is bowing ourselves down and acknowledging that only One is worthy. As we can see from Abraham's life, worship and obedience go hand in hand. You cannot say that you are worshiping the Lord while being disobedient to Him at the same time.

From the Bible, we can find several expressions of worship that bring a bigger meaning to the definitions we got in the paragraph above. Here are just a few of them:

Giving

Matthew 6:21 "for where your treasure is, there your heart will be also."

Serving

Rom 1:9a "For God is my witness, whom I serve with my spirit in the gospel of His Son."

2 Tim 1:3a "I thank God, whom I serve with a pure conscience."

Speaking

Psalm 34:1 "I will bless the Lord at all times: His praise shall continually be in my mouth."

Shouting

Psalm 27:6b "at His tabernacle will I sacrifice with shouts of joy;"

Singing

Psalm 47:6 "Sing praises to God, sing praises: Sing ye praises with understanding."

Bowing

Ps 95:6 "O come let us bow down: Let us kneel before the Lord our Maker."

Standing

Psalm 33:8 "Let all the earth fear the Lord; Let all the inhabitants of the world stand in awe of Him."

Dancing

Psalm 149:3 "let them praise His name in the dance."

Playing Instruments

Psalm 33:2 "praise the Lord with the harp: and an instrument of ten strings."

Clapping

Psalm 47:1 "O clap your hands all ye people; shout unto God with the voice of triumph."

Lifting hands

Psalm 63:4b "I will lift up my hands in Thy name."

Now that we have an idea of the different expressions of worship, we will be using all of them and more in the course of the book.

WHY We Worship

We worship because HE IS WORTHY!

Right now the Lord has His throne surrounded by continuous worship. The angels, twenty-four elders and the four living beings bow before Him night and day saying *Holy, Holy, Holy is the Lord God Almighty*; *The whole earth is full of His glory*. Revelation 4:2-11 gives us a clear picture of what happens in heaven on a daily basis.

But if the Lord has all this going for Him, why does He still desire to see the same thing here on earth? It is because the relationship between God and man is very important to Him. We are created in His image and His greatest desire is for us to live in His presence. As we see in Genesis 1:26-28 where it says, *"then God said, "Let Us make man in Our image, according to Our likeness; let them have dominion over the fish of the sea, over the birds of the air, and over the cattle, over all the earth and over every creeping thing that creeps on the earth." So God created man in His own image; in the image of God He created him; male and female He created them. Then God blessed them and God said to them, "Be fruitful and multiply; fill the earth and subdue it; have dominion over the fish of the sea, over the birds of the air, and over every living thing that moves on the earth."*

We were created to worship. Why would God create us to worship when He has angels and cherubim and seraphim to worship Him? This is because the worship that these beings offer Him is by designation and not by will. So God wanted to create somebody different that does not worship Him because they have to, but because they want to.

Before the fall of man, Lucifer was the one in charge of worship. His job was to cover God in worship. Every instrument was in him and he filled heaven with the best sound ever heard. Lucifer means the bearer of light which meant that the light of God emanated through him. He was very beautiful! He became proud, exalted himself and started thinking that *he was the object of worship.* He was so impressed with his own beauty and position that he wanted the glory that belongs to God alone. He began to *want the worship that he was created to offer to God.* He ended up being thrown out of heaven by Michael the Archangel. So, there was a vacancy and God created man to fill the place that Lucifer lost. But why man? Man can sin. Man can also choose not to worship. God understood that worship that is offered willingly is far greater in value than worship that is offered by design. He gave us a choice to look at everything He had created and search for ourselves and see that there is no God like Him in all the earth and then after all this say, *"I will bless the Lord at all times, His praise shall continually be in my mouth!"*

The fall of Lucifer

Ezekiel 28:1-11says "Moreover the word of the Lord came to me, saying, "Son of man, take up a lamentation for the king of Tyre, and say to him, 'Thus says the Lord God:

> *"You were the seal of perfection,*
> *Full of wisdom and perfect in beauty.*
> *You were in Eden, the garden of God;*
> *Every precious stone was your covering:*
> *The sardius, topaz, and diamond,*

Beryl, onyx, and jasper,
Sapphire, turquoise, and emerald with gold.
The workmanship of your timbrels and pipes
Was prepared for you on the day you were created.

"You were the anointed cherub who covers;
I established you;
You were on the holy mountain of God;
You walked back and forth in the midst of fiery stones.
You were perfect in your ways from the day you were created,
Till iniquity was found in you.

"By the abundance of your trading
You became filled with violence within,
And you sinned;
Therefore I cast you as a profane thing
Out of the mountain of God;
And I destroyed you, O covering cherub,
From the midst of the fiery stones.

"Your heart was lifted up because of your beauty;
You corrupted your wisdom for the sake of your splendor;
I cast you to the ground,
I laid you before kings,
That they might gaze at you.

"You defiled your sanctuaries
By the multitude of your iniquities,
By the iniquity of your trading;
Therefore I brought fire from your midst;

It devoured you,
And I turned you to ashes upon the earth
In the sight of all who saw you.
All who knew you among the peoples are astonished at you;
You have become a horror,
And shall be no more forever."

Because of sin, man was separated from God but God still wanted relationship with us. And still does. He is madly in love with us and this is why He sent His only Son Jesus Christ to redeem us and to restore us into the presence of God that was lost in the Garden of Eden due to disobedience. God wants His family back! We also find ourselves purposeless unless we are in the presence of God because this is what we were created for. To share a Spirit to spirit relationship with the Lord. This is why there's a yearning in your soul. You know and can feel that there is more than just running in circles exhausted and ending up emptier than you were before you began. You are right! You will only find fulfilment in the pursuit of God because we were created to worship.

So, when we begin to do what is being done in heaven right here on earth, an *ordinary* room becomes a *throne room*. When we worship on earth as it is in heaven, heaven and earth come together and God releases Himself to us.

Worshiping the Lord is not just about us experiencing His presence. It is about us loving Him too. It is us putting Him first on our hearts as He says in the first commandment. Matthew 2:3-37 says, *"then one of them, a lawyer, asked Him a question, testing Him and saying, "Teacher, which is the great commandment in the law?" Jesus said to him, "You shall love the Lord your God with all your heart, with all your soul, and with all your mind,' this is the first and great commandment."*

He wants to be with us and be loved by us. He craves your love. This is how we minister to Him. Our love can ravish His heart. Even when you feel that your love is weak, it is real love to Him and He appreciates it. Imperfect, but highly valued! He desires fellowship with us. To walk in unity with us, like He did in the Garden of Eden. It is only now that we work hard to get into His presence but this was not always the case. God's original plan for us was that we do everything with Him. Had Adam not sinned, we would not have to work ourselves through singing or playing instruments as we see in the Garden of Eden.

God could have put His throne anywhere, but He chose to put it in imperfect people- in their praises. He is obsessed with us. The Message bible says in Psalm 22:3 *"He is leaning back on the cushions of Israel's praise"* which means that he finds a resting place. Worship is about Jesus finding a resting place where He can abide. This is why He is seeking worshipers and this goes to explain why worshipers are like magnets to the heart and presence of the Lord. When He is invited to take the throne of our hearts' affections, praises etc. He finds a resting place in us. Purposing to live your life in such a way that *"Lord, Your presence finds a resting place in my life. I want you to feel so at home in my life."* It takes first priority in my life. Give yourself to this. When you worship you pull the throne of heaven into the earth realm and Jesus becomes enthroned in that place or situation and when the King comes, He brings His kingdom with Him. It sums up His desire to find a place on earth where He can put His presence again. This is why He loves available vessels that love Him back and want to allow Him to have a resting place in them. Let's value spending long hours with Jesus.

Worship is the main attraction! It is our job description. We always become like the One we worship.

I challenge you to stop right now and acknowledge the Lord wherever you are. Enthrone Him in that place. David says in psalm 119:164 (Message Bible), "Seven *times each day I stop and shout praises.*" Imagine this was a man who was leading a whole nation and was always on the frontline of battle. But even in that busy schedule, He stopped seven times each day to shout praises unto the Lord! All his workers must have known this and I believe that they too, joined their king since what the King did was pleasing to all people. You see, when you go to work, you don't have to leave the Lord at home or in your car because you are afraid that you won't have time or the environment is not so good for Him. The only thing you need to do is to acknowledge Him like David. And in that very moment your office becomes a throne room. You don't have to wait for big worship experiences or your Sunday service for this. You can have this every minute of your life. This helps you not to have any breaks in your worship such that you are worshiping the Lord continually even in busy schedules. You don't need an hour to accomplish this. If ten minutes is all you have, make the best of those ten minutes.

I practice the presence of the Lord everywhere. I have decided to make it the chief part of my life. I work in a pretty busy environment and I have developed a habit of quieting myself completely (while still working amongst my coworkers who can be loud) and set my gaze on the Lord. Sometimes His presence will be so overwhelming and I can't hold my tears but I choose to focus on Him even as I work. In this crazy environment, the Holy Spirit has given me several songs but because I have centered my spirit upon Him, I did not lose the words or the tune He gave me. It is possible to live in worship twenty four seven! Even when you are going through the valley, stop and acknowledge Him, stop and shout praises to Him and as the Bible says in Psalm 2:9b, *"You shall dash them to pieces like a potter's vessel)."* Whatever it is that you're going through, when you start to enthrone Him, He dashes it into pieces. Oh hallelujah! What a mighty God we serve!

Can you imagine what David would do if he lived in the age we are living in? This is what he always longed for! Not being separated from the presence of the Lord and that he could enter in at any moment. We don't have to do any blood sacrifices like He had to in his time. Jesus has given the ultimate sacrifice and the veil has been torn and we can now go in for ourselves. My friend, take advantage of this opportunity we have been given.

David had a clear understanding of WHO God is and because of this; He was able to worship Him right. We must know what we believe before we offer our praise because it is not enough to offer our worship before we know Who we praise. My worship is determined by my view of God. If my view of Him is less than Who He is, then the worship that I offer Him is not adequate for the being that I praise. I must know who He is so that when I worship Him, what I say about Him is befitting the dignity of His Being. We have to have a proper view of God before we can worship. He says in Psalm 34:3, *"Oh, magnify the Lord with me, and let us exalt His name together."* How can we magnify God? How can we make an already big God bigger than He already is? Just think about a magnifying glass and an object that you can't see that you want to examine. You have to change the magnification of the lens so that you can magnify it to make it bigger. You really are not making it bigger, but your perception of it makes it bigger. So then, same case applies about magnifying God. How you see Him gets bigger. In whatever you're going through, your view of Him gets bigger and bigger. The more you magnify Him in your life, the more your perception of Him changes.

On my personal progression into worship, the cry of my heart has been to be wrecked with a hunger so great, to be fully possessed by God and be distinguished by His Presence. For this, I have made up my mind over the years to seek Him with all my heart and to be an eternal dwelling place for Him. I am willing to pay every price for this. He is not an unjust God; He will fulfill the desire of they that diligently seek Him. He will be found by them.

A lot has happened along the way. Some things I expected, but others came as a surprise to me. But one thing I was sure about is that the hand of God was in it otherwise, I would not have made it out. The word of God in *Romans 8:2 says, "All things work together for good to those who love God, to those who are the called according to His purpose."* What this means is that, the good, bad and ugly are all put together to produce a good finished product in our lives even though it doesn't look like it right now. When these things happen to you, they do not mean any good to you; In fact, the intention of the enemy of your soul is that he crushes you through everything that you go through. But thanks be unto God who causes us to triumph in Christ Jesus! He uses everything that was meant for evil to bring out the best in and through us.

In Psalm 119:71, David says that *it is good that he has been afflicted, that he may learn the statutes of the Lord.* In the same Psalm on verse 92 he says that *"unless Your law had been my delight, I would then have perished in my affliction."* This means that while he was getting afflicted, he learned how to focus on the law of the Lord which kept him from perishing.

Let me give you a little background into my life and progression. I was born and raised in Kenya by my dear parents Angelica and Peter Muiruri. I am the first born of seven children – three boys and four girls. My parents are ministers of the gospel. My mom is a worship leader and my dad is a pastor, so I grew up in the church. I started by singing in the kids worship team as a child and singing for guests at our house along with my sisters. Dad would always call us out to sing to the guests and we did it joyfully. However, I wouldn't learn about worship until later when I was around ten years old. My dad and I are very close and much of the relationship that I have with the Lord I learned from him. He unknowingly taught me about worship. As a little girl, I used to go to him every day like all kids do and just ask for stuff. "Daddy, I want this! Daddy, do this for me!" And I would get an attitude when he didn't do it for me. Then one day, after dad came home from work, we began to chat. He was very tired and I as a child, just wanted to chat. So I went and sat next to him and he told me that in that state in which he was, exhausted from work, that I should as his child seek to know how I can make his day better instead of fussing about things he didn't get for me. I was listening intently and because I love my dad dearly, I asked him how

I could do that. He said, talk to me and find out how my day was and ask me if there is any way you can make it better. My dad is a mechanic when he is not preaching so, when he came home sometimes, his shoes would be full of oil from the cars he was repairing all day.

In my childish way, I said "*aha! I will be cleaning daddy's shoes when he comes home and I will wash his feet too.*" So I started doing this every night. By the time dad was sitting comfortably in his chair, I had warm water and soap and was at his feet washing his feet and then go out and clean his shoes all this time without asking him for anything. I was getting very excited just seeing how happy that made him. While I was doing this, another one of my siblings would be massaging his head. It was now after doing this that I noticed dad is the one that was asking me what I wanted, and he would say things like, *"whatever it is, I will get it for you"*. At this point, my life had changed, and I found myself going out of my way to please dad and get so happy as I watched him wonder what he would get me this time around. It wasn't until when I was thirteen years old when the Lord called me that I understood why I was doing what I was doing to dad. It is the same thing I was doing to the Lord when I sang and sang to Him for hours outside our house and just be so happy when I put a smile on His face. He was always there to listen and receive.

I grew up loving the Lord with my whole heart after going through a lot of crazy stuff in my early years. I knew Him as **the One who was always there**. I always felt that I was being followed by this friend who was ready to listen to me any time and who would bring a lot of shame to my enemies, causing me to laugh and cry in joy so much as I watched the things meant to destroy me backfire.

His presence was very real to me and I knew every time He walked in His fullness into a room, no matter how dark the situation was. I remember standing outside our house every night while I sung to Him with all my heart, tears streaming down my face and the whisper from Him to sing it again as He listened to my ministry to Him as a young girl. I always knew that He loved me; oh how He loved me and that He wanted to be with me! Nobody could take that away from me. It is from these experiences with Him as a little girl that I learned how to host and entertain Him with my worship.

I had experienced so much rejection in my earlier days especially at school and this somehow taught me to always run to the Lord. I did not care who stayed or who left because I had come to know WHO was always there with me. I did not mind spending lots of hours by myself up to this day because I was never really alone. Most worshipers go through a lot of rejection in their lives and it is through this that they learn to always run to the Lord. When someone has gone through so much rejection, they sort of expect people to leave or act up and this can cause a cold heart within you. You have to continually surrender to the Lord and know that He is for you no matter what. As for me, my Lord was mine and no one could tell Him anything about me that would cause Him to reject me, because as a matter of fact, when I grew up I came to know that He loved me in all my weaknesses and His strength was made perfect in me. The powerful thing about the strength of the Lord being made perfect in us is that in times of your weaknesses when the enemy longs to expose your nakedness, the Lord covers you in that area with His strength such that people will not see it but rather experience the grace and power of God upon you.

I knew the hand of the Lord was upon my life even because of the unusual things I found myself in and how He would show up on the scene and pull me out. It's like He was trying to make a statement through my life. She is Mine! The Lord is a mighty warrior. The Bible calls Him a Mighty Man of war. As the storms of life threw me all over the place, I trusted the hand of He who was controlling them and watched Him deliver me with such fervor. He is a very jealous God. He moves in like a jealous husband over His bride, burning up everything that is coming in between Him and her. I remember how sometimes the storms would be so intense that I would often wonder if I'd make it out at that particular time but with each intense storm, came intense glory afterwards. Romans 8:18 says, *"For I consider that the sufferings of this present time are not worthy to be compared with the glory which will be revealed in us."*

What I didn't know in depth at my young age was how the Lord loved my worship and how he was molding me into someone who would later teach others about it through the things that I had suffered. I had to go through all the pain and rejection so that I could only have One Person to look to – Jesus. As Paul would say in 1 Corinthians 2:3-4, *"Blessed be the God and Father of our Lord Jesus Christ, the Father of all comfort, who comforts us in all our tribulation, that we may be able to comfort those who are in any trouble, with the comfort which we ourselves are comforted by God."* I was comforted so that I may comfort today and teach the same principles that I was taught by the Lord on my personal journey.

My worship went higher and higher as I progressed in life, and every season the Lord would reveal a different facet of Himself that I hadn't known in the previous one as my heart yearned for Him and I sought Him with all my strength, longing for that which only He could give.

The rivers in my heart bubbled and flowed and refreshed, and quenched my thirst over and over again, as He cleansed me and to this day, there is no place I'd rather be than in His presence. It is where I belong! I was made for His presence. Nothing can take me out of this place. No one can kick me out of His presence. I will dwell here all the days of my life. No power of hell can chase me out of here. I have made the Lord my abode and I will dwell in His presence all the days off my life. Ps 26:8 says, *"Lord, I have loved the habitation of Your house and the place where Your glory dwells.*

CHAPTER TWO

The Worshipers Role:

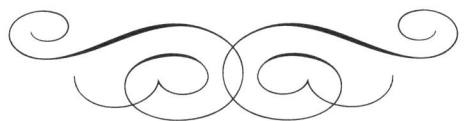

Our main role as worshipers is to minister to the Lord. Ministry to the Lord is the highest calling of a worshiper. It is our duty to oversee worship and as we do this, we also have in mind that our allotted inheritance is the Lord Himself. He is to be the focus of our service, the Source of our sustenance and the significance of our calling. With all this in mind, this is where we move beyond just singing or leading people into worship to a one on one encounter with our Lord. You are worshiping Him as you remember what He told Abraham in Genesis 15:1b *"Do not be afraid, Abram. I am your shield, your exceedingly great reward."* Our reward is only found in the Lord! He is the reward!

When we worship the Lord with the revelation of this word that ***He is the reward***, our worship will shift to a very high dimension because we are no longer looking at man to recognize us or thank us since we already know WHO our reward is, and when the Lord gives you Himself, you will never want for anything!

Suddenly, we find ourselves at His feet, bathing His feet with our tears and wiping them with our hair. During a service, it is not unusual for worship leaders to give a word of encouragement time or lead songs on encouragement, but what I found out is that when you minister to the Lord and cast all your cares and those of the congregation upon Him as He has asked us to in His word, it gets so much easier because you as the worship leader will not have to "force" a word to come out of you, but the Lord Himself will minister to His own people. *Vertical ministry will always lead to horizontal ministry.* I don't know about you, but this is so much easier to me! John 12:32 says, "*If I be lifted up above the earth, I will draw all men unto Myself.*" If we lift Him up, He will deliver, heal and restore His children. We don't have to "work" it. Very many worship leaders have come to this point of exhaustion in the course of their ministry because they failed to grasp this simple truth that our first mission is to lift Jesus higher and higher and let Him do all the delivering, touching and healing. They worked themselves into a serious exhaustion and end up angry at God or the church because they felt "*used or burnt out*". The Lord does not use like man uses.

When you've been used by the Lord, you will feel used but the one difference between Him and man is that it is a different kind of "*use*". He replenishes you after He uses you and you feel fulfillment and purpose unlike where you feel empty after being used by man. This is why it is so important to go back at His feet after leading worship so that He can fill you. After pouring out so much of yourself while ministering, you are left vulnerable and this is the most opportune time for the enemy to attack. Most of the times, after a great victory, ministers find themselves getting attacked by the enemy of our souls in what we call backlash or retaliation. He doesn't wait for later because he knows that you're vulnerable at that particular time after such a mighty ministry and comes after you in retaliation. I've had numerous cases where worship leaders thought something was wrong with them because of the kind of attacks that they found themselves in after a great victory. When we are too busy celebrating the victory, the enemy is busy planning his retaliation on you. You have to run to the Lord immediately and ask Him to fill you up in every way that you ministered that day and then you can celebrate. It is also wise to have your pastor cover you in prayer after such a feat. This shuts the door of vulnerability in the Spirit and ensures that you're totally covered.

Often times, as I worship and lead, I find myself at the feet of my Lord with Him yearning for my deepest worship. He provokes me in a way that causes me to erupt in ministry to Him. His depth calls out to my depth and the Holy Spirit hovers all over me as He helps me exalt Jesus. And then the most beautiful thing happens, I see Him minister not only to the congregation but me as well. Psalm 42:7 says, *"Deep calls unto deep at the noise of Your waterfalls; All Your waves and billows have gone over me."* It is the most beautiful place! I cannot explain the exhilaration I feel as my spirit soars through His Spirit, and as I call Him *"Holy!"* It is like nothing I have ever seen or heard before. I could be in a public place leading worship, but at the same time, I am all alone with Him in His private chambers and He is touching His children according to their need and me too. What a mighty God we serve! He is the only God who is able to touch and reveal Himself to us all at the same time in one seating in different ways. He becomes healing to one, deliverance to the other, salvation to one, and encouragement to another.

My main goal is to saturate the Lord with my worship such that He will have no other option than to move upon my worship and touch His people, myself included. It is possible to infuse the Maker of this world with the very thing that He longs for the most – Worship. Yes, the angels and elders worship Him twenty four seven, but He has put such value on His children that He longs for our worship so much that even the angels marvel. (new sentence) In Psalms 8:4 the Bible says, "*What is man, that thou art mindful of him? And the son of man, that thou visitest him?*" It is our worship that He looks forward to and the only thing that the Maker of the earth seeks.

Worship is a lifestyle of oneness with God. It is not a thirty minute thing on Sunday morning nor is it a slow song or a hymn. We looked at different expressions of worship from the Bible earlier. It is union and communion with God where you and He become one. It is a relationship where you make good of Him and intentionally spend time with Him privately before you get on the stages of man. As a matter of fact, what happens in public stages must be an overflow of what happens in your secret place with the Lord. You must have your own personal altar where you seek Him from and then out of that fullness go out. This means it's not a last minute thing you're doing just because your pastor asked you to lead this Sunday and then now is the time you're dusting your Bible and closet to seek the Lord! No, you stay prepared in His presence continuously ministering to Him. You have to be in pursuit of God. The same way we hate being used is the same way He does. Seek Him out of love for Him!

Make up your mind this day to go after Him seriously shunning every distraction. There are so many things crying out for our attention in this age! We have become so inundated with information such that focus is almost a foreign word to many. You will experience many distractions when you make up your mind to go after the Lord but don't lose heart, keep going after the Lover of your soul. If you fall, don't condemn yourself, get back up and run after Him. It is not in vain!

I do not want you to think that I am writing this book because I have it all together, No! I have to re-commit to the Lord over and over again after getting distracted. Sometimes I will not realize that I am distracted until the Holy Spirit nudges me and at that point I run back into the arms of my Father. You see, getting distracted is not a sin; the sin is in knowing you are distracted and not doing anything about it thus continuing in the distraction. The Lord does not have a probationary period for us as His children. This means that the moment you find yourself distracted, all you need to do is get back on your feet and recommit to seeking His face again. This is the heart of David and the Lord loves it!

When you get ready to go after the Lord, be prepared for a stripping off of everything that is a distraction. Hebrews 12:1 says, "*lay aside every weight and the sin that does so easily beset us, so we can run with patience the race that's set before us.*" You will not be able to go after Him fully with these weights. You see, weights don't necessarily keep you from running. They keep you from running well and the truth is, no one has to tell you what hinders you; you already know! What demands that you spend your time with it more than you do with God? Is it a person? Search your heart and lay aside the things that have somehow crept in and taken a prominent place in your heart. Our God is a jealous God who demands that we lay aside all that crowds Him out.

You have to get to a place and say like Paul in Philippians 3:7-9, *"But what things were gain to me, these I have counted loss for Christ. Yet indeed I also count all things loss for the excellence off the knowledge of Christ Jesus my Lord, for whom I have suffered the loss of all things, and count them as rubbish, that I may gain Christ and be found in Him, not having my own righteousness, which is from the law, but that which is through faith in Christ, the righteousness which is from God by faith; that I may know Him."* At first he said that he "*counted*" all the things loss for the knowledge of Christ and then as he continued to change "*count*" which means that it's something he had to do on a daily basis. What are you holding onto that hinders your intimacy with the Lord? You have to count it as dung and Jesus as your treasure and priority. Please take a moment and examine your heart.

Nothing else will satisfy the longing in your heart! What's wrong with you is that your thirst has not been quenched. There is a big conversation about water but nobody drinks. We all get online and talk about how hungry and thirsty we are for the Lord and want to know Him more but we are not doing the work that calls for it. We even talk about it around our dinner tables but we do not go after the real thirst quencher as we ought to. So it becomes just another fantasy.

Real worship is born out of thirst!

Psalm 63:1-8 says

"O God, You are my God; early will I seek You; My soul thirsts for You; My flesh longs for You in a dry and thirsty land where there is no water. So I have looked for You in the sanctuary, to see Your power and Your glory. Because Your lovingkindness is better than life, My lips shall praise You. Thus I will bless You while I live; I will lift up my hands in Your name. My soul shall be satisfied as with marrow and fatness, and my mouth shall praise You with joyful lips. When I remember You on my bed, I meditate on You in the night watches. Because You have been my help, therefore in the shadow of Your wings I will rejoice. My soul follows close behind You; Your right hand upholds me."

David lets us know that it is in only blessing the Lord and seeking His face that our souls are satisfied as with marrow and fatness. This means that when we satisfy His longing to be worshiped by us, He in turn satisfies our souls and fills every void so that we are no longer wanting for anything else to fill us up. You are not addicted to that thing that you think you are addicted to, your soul is crying out for God. That's why no matter how much of it you have, you are never satisfied. You keep going back for more because your spirit man is trying to pass a message to you and your body is manifesting it through that appetite. Your soul has an appetite and it is for God. It gets expressed in different ways in our bodies but that language is translated into hunger and thirst for the Lord who is the only one that can bring fulfilment to us.

David was in the wilderness of Judah. So, getting thirsty in such parched desert conditions is to be expected. It is the next verse that lets us know that he understood that what he needed was more than natural water and that as he blesses the Lord and worships Him, his soul gets satisfied in the process. The word *marrow* here is *cheleb* in Hebrew which means *richest or choice part* and fatness means abundance which represents the fatty ashes of sacrifices. The fatness was a result of the sacrifices of animals on the altar which the Mosaic Law prohibited people from eating because it belonged to God alone. Leviticus 3:16 says, *"It is the food of the offering made by fire for a sweet savor: all **the fat is the Lord's.**"*

Marrow is the nourisher and strengthener of the bones; it is said to moisten the bones. Thus, the expression is used figuratively of the things which alone can satisfy the soul. So, in short, what David is saying here is that *"Lord, when I bless Your name in worship, You will satisfy me with the richest and choice part of fatness (abundance)!"* It can also be translated into *"fatness"*. What a wonderful thing that the Lord will fill us with the fatness of His fatness! You definitely wouldn't go looking for anything else to fill you up after such an encounter.

As we have seen above, our soul is always looking for satisfaction and now that we have established that only God can satisfy and fill us up, let us look closely at the scripture again, David acknowledges that God is his God and how his soul thirsted for Him. He paints us a picture of how parched it feels in the place where he is in the wilderness of Judah. This is the same Judean desert where he grew up as a shepherd boy. So in essence, he knew where all the seasonal springs and waterholes were and he would have gone for it better yet, send someone to fetch some water for him. Yet his language here makes us see that it is something more he was longing for and not just natural water. He was longing for God.

"Give me this water that I may not thirst nor come here to draw."

John 4: 2-24 says, "So *He came to a city of Samaria which is called Sychar, near the plot of ground that Jacob gave to his son Joseph. Now Jacob's well was there. Jesus therefore, being wearied from His journey, sat thus by the well. It was about the sixth hour. A woman of Samaria came to draw water. Jesus said to her, "Give Me a drink. "For His disciples had gone away into the city to buy food. Then the woman of Samaria said to Him, "How is it that You, being a Jew, ask a drink from me, a Samaritan woman?" For Jews have no dealings with Samaritans. Jesus answered and said to her, "If you knew the gift of God, and who it is who says to you, 'Give Me a drink,' you would have asked Him, and He would have given you living water." The woman said to Him, "Sir, You have nothing to draw with, and the well is deep. Where then do You get that living water? Are You greater than our father Jacob, who gave us the well, and drank from it himself, as well as his sons and his livestock?" Jesus answered and said to her, "Whoever drinks of this water will thirst again, but whoever drinks of the water that I shall give him will never thirst. But the water that I shall give him will become in him a fountain of water springing up into everlasting life." The woman said to Him, "Sir, give me this water, that I may not thirst, nor come here to draw." Jesus said to her, "Go, call your husband, and come here." The woman answered and said, "I have no husband." Jesus said to her, "You have well said, 'I have no husband,' for you have had five husbands, and the one whom you now have is not your husband; in that you spoke truly." The woman said to Him, "Sir, I perceive that You are a* prophet. *Our fathers worshiped on this mountain, and you Jews say that in Jerusalem is the place where one ought to worship.*"

Jesus said to her, "Woman, believe Me, the hour is coming when you will neither on this mountain, nor in Jerusalem, worship the Father. You worship what you do not know; we know what we worship, for salvation is of the Jews. But the hour is coming, and now is, when the true worshipers will worship the Father in spirit and truth; for the Father is seeking such to worship Him. God is Spirit, and those who worship Him must worship in spirit and truth."

In the above passage Jesus said to the Samaritan woman that the Father is **seeking** for those who worship Him in Spirit and truth. The word **seeking** here means to search for something hidden until you find it or to go after something, like how a thirsty animal seeks for the water he can smell. It is out of this thirst that the Lord seeks out a worshiper. He is thirsty for the worship that they offer Him in truth and in Spirit. He will stop at nothing until He gets to them!

This tells me how powerful true worship is; that when I open my mouth in Spirit and in truth I am no longer the *hunter* but I become the *hunted*. Do you see how powerful this is? The Lord, the Maker of the universe, seeks me just like I am seeking Him in my worship. It is like a Divine exchange. I can almost see Him in my wild imagination, sprinting out of His throne as the angels look in amazement wondering, "What now?" and Michael the archangel is ready to act as he thinks his services must be needed on this one until he realizes how the heart of the Lord is bubbling in joy and His face radiating with gladness as

He exclaims, "She is worshiping Me! Just look at her worshiping me in Spirit and truth. I have found her!"

I have found this to be very true about worship. That in one moment I could be in a situation where all I am craving is the manifest presence of God, and instead of striving and calling Him there, the Lord revealed to me the secret of worship that I have the ability to move His heart and engulf myself in His presence. In one second, I was crying for His manifest presence, but in the other second, when I lifted my hands in Spirit and truth, He sought me out and wanted to be where I was - Where He was being glorified. Healings and deliverances happen here most of the times without having to lay hands on anyone. Divine provisions happen here, when you decide to take your eyes off of whatever you're going through and just tell Him, "*Lord, You are wonderful!*"

It is in this realm that the Lord meets all of our needs as we meet His. Whatever you are looking for, you can worship your way into it. This does not mean worshiping in manipulation (The Lord knows our motives anyway). It means that you stop striving about what your desires are and concentrate totally on the Lord and then He will move on your behalf. It is a place of no selfishness, where all your being is saying, **"I am here to glorify you and not my problem!"**. Being driven by His faithfulness and mercy towards us.

2 Chronicles 16:9 says, "For *the eyes of the Lord run to and fro throughout the whole earth, to show Himself strong on behalf of those whose heart is loyal to Him.*" And once He finds even one person that has set their heart to please Him, He sets His mark upon them.

Beloved, the Lord is hungry for your worship and when you learn how to fill Him up first even in moments where you might feel that you're depleted, He will fill you up with Himself. This reminds me of the story in the Bible about Elijah and the widow. 1 Kings 17:7-16 says, *"Sometime later the brook dried up because there had been no rain in the land. Then the word of the Lord came to him: "Go at once to Zarephath in the region of Sidon and stay there. I have directed a widow there to supply you with food." So he went to Zarephath. When he came to the town gate, a widow was there gathering sticks. He called to her and asked, "Would you bring me a little water in a jar so I may have a drink?" As she was going to get it, he called, "And bring me, please, a piece of bread." "As surely as the Lord your God lives," she replied, "I don't have any bread—only a handful of flour in a jar and a little olive oil in a jug. I am gathering a few sticks to take home and make a meal for myself and my son, that we may eat it—and die. "Elijah said to her "Don't be afraid. Go home and do as you have said. But first make a small loaf of bread for me from what you have and bring it to me, and then make something for yourself and your son. For this is what the Lord, the God of Israel, says: 'The jar of flour will not be used up and the jug of oil will not run dry until the day the Lord sends rain on the land.' "She went away and did as Elijah had told her. So there was food every day for Elijah and for the woman and her family. For the jar of flour was not used up and the jug of oil did not run dry, in keeping with the word of the Lord spoken by Elijah."*

To the common sense, the prophet here seems to be an unfair selfish man who cared only about himself by asking for what the poor widow who was preparing her last meal for herself and her son so that they could eat and the die. But when she obeyed and trusted the word of the prophet, her life was changed completely. And this is the same thing with us. The same principle about putting the prophet first applies here. Common sense does not apply in real worship. For it is when we fill Jesus up first with our worship and praise that He causes there to be an overflow in our lives of the things that we need. Common sense will tell you to take care of yourself first when you're hungry and thirsty, but even in your lowest moments, if you learn how to fill Jesus up, He will make sure you are taken care of. Even in pain, learn to put yourself aside and give Him the last drop of your worship. He will make sure you are taken care of. I know what I'm talking about!

True worship also demands that you have an audacity. Matthew 15:21-28 says, *"Then Jesus went out from there and departed to the region of Tyre and Sidon. And behold, a woman of Canaan came from that region and cried out to Him, saying, "Have mercy on me, O Lord, Son of David! My daughter is severely demon-possessed. "But He answered her not a word. And His disciples came and urged Him, saying, "Send her away, for she cries out after us. "But He answered and said, "I was not sent except to the lost sheep of the house of Israel. "Then she came and worshiped Him, saying, "Lord, help me! "But He answered and said, "It is not good to take the children's bread and throw it to the little dogs. "And she said, "Yes, Lord, yet even the little dogs eat the crumbs which fall from their masters' table. "Then Jesus answered and said to her, "O woman, great is your faith! Let it be to you as you desire."* And her daughter was healed from that very hour.

Worship is not for the weak in heart. As we see from the passage above, we see that Jesus kept dismissing her and even insulted her at some point but undeterred, she kept worshiping until He had no other option than to do for her what she had petitioned Him. Her desperation and worship made Him respond to her.

CHAPTER THREE

"Detaining" The Lord with Our worship

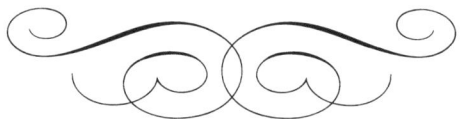

Another very important role of the worshiper is to "detain" the Lord until worship turns into *communication*, *fellowship* and then *intercession*. You're probably wondering how it is possible to "detain" the Lord in worship. Yes, it is possible and biblical too. I often tell worshipers and worship leaders alike that when they lead worship or are in an individual moment of worship and the glory is manifest, often times the enemy will cause us to rush out or finish the worship prematurely because of our programs and schedules. In doing this, we curtail so much of what is happening in the Spirit that we cannot see with our bare eyes and end up quenching the Spirit of the living God. Lay there and wait on Him for a while and see what He has to say!

Let's look at Abraham's example in Genesis Chapter 18:1- 33.

"Then the Lord appeared to him by the terebinth trees of Mamre, as he was sitting in the tent door in the heat of the day. So he lifted his eyes and looked, and behold, three men were standing by him; and when he saw them, he ran from the tent door to meet them, and bowed himself to the ground, and said, "My Lord, if I have now found favor in Your sight, do not pass on by Your servant. Please let a little water be brought, and wash your feet, and rest yourselves under the tree. And I will bring a morsel of bread, that you may refresh your hearts. After that you may pass by, inasmuch as you have come to your servant. "They said, "Do as you have said. "So Abraham hurried into the tent to Sarah and said, "Quickly, make ready three measures of fine meal; knead it and make cakes." And Abraham ran to the herd, took a tender and good calf, gave it to a young man, and he hastened to prepare it. So he took butter and milk and the calf which he had prepared, and set it before them; and he stood by them under the tree as they ate. Then they said to him, "Where is Sarah your wife? "So he said, "Here, in the tent. "And He said, "I will certainly return to you according to the time of life, and behold, Sarah your wife shall have a son."(Sarah was listening in the tent door which was behind him.) Now Abraham and Sarah were old, well advanced in age; and Sarah had passed the age of childbearing. Therefore, Sarah laughed within herself, saying, "After I have grown old, shall I have pleasure, my lord being old also? "And the Lord said to Abraham, "Why did Sarah laugh, saying, 'Shall I surely bear a child, since I am old?' Is anything too hard for the Lord? At the appointed time I will return to you, according to the time of life, and Sarah shall have a son." But Sarah denied it, saying, "I did not laugh," for she was afraid. And He said, "No, but you did laugh! "Then the men rose

from there and looked toward Sodom, and Abraham went with them to send them on the way. And the Lord said, "Shall I hide from Abraham what I am doing, since Abraham shall surely become a great and mighty nation, and all the nations of the earth shall be blessed in him? For I have known him, in order that he may command his children and his house-hold after him, that they keep the way of the Lord, to do righteousness and justice, that the Lord may bring to Abraham what He has spoken to him." And the Lord said, "Because the outcry against Sodom and Gomorrah is great, and because their sin is very grave, I will go down now and see whether they have done altogether according to the outcry against it that has come to Me; and if not, I will know."

Then the men turned away from there and went toward Sodom, but Abraham still stood before the Lord. And Abraham came near and said, "Would You also destroy the righteous with the wicked? Suppose there were fifty righteous within the city; would You also destroy the place and not spare it for the fifty righteous that were in it? Far be it from You to do such a thing as this, to slay the righteous with the wicked, so that the righteous should be as the wicked; far be it from You! Shall not the Judge of all the earth do right? "So, the Lord said, "If I find in Sodom fifty righteous within the city, then I will spare all the place for their sakes. "Then Abraham answered and said, "Indeed now, I who am but dust and ashes have taken it upon myself to speak to the Lord: Suppose there were five less than the fifty righteous; would You destroy all of the city for lack of five?"

So He said, "If I find there forty-five, I will not destroy it." And he spoke to Him yet again and said, "Suppose there should be forty found there?" So He said, "I will not do it for the sake of forty." Then he said, "Let not the Lord be angry, and I will speak: Suppose thirty should be found there?" So

He said, "I will not do it if I find thirty there." And he said, "Indeed now, I have taken it upon myself to speak to the Lord: Suppose twenty should be found there? "So He said, "I will not destroy it for the sake of twenty." Then he said, "Let not the Lord be angry, and I will speak but once more: Suppose ten should be found there?" And He said, "I will not destroy it for the sake of ten." So the Lord went His way as soon as He had finished speaking with Abraham; and Abraham returned to his place."

In this scripture we see how Abraham ran to the Lord and bowed down to Him. As we saw earlier, one of the expressions used in worship is bowing down. It is a way of showing the highest reverence to some-one or something. Abraham was resting under the terebinth trees and when he looked up, he saw that the Lord had appeared to him and his first reaction was running towards Him and bowing at His feet.

Abraham, who is also called the friend of God, knew how rare such an occasion was and he decided to maximize it by being hospitable to the Lord. In those days, he understood that it's not every day that the Lord came by your house. Instead of taking it for granted, though he was communicating with the Lord every so often, he knew that the Lord does not just visit with no agenda on His mind. I can almost hear Him say to Himself, *"I will detain Him until I find out what is on His mind!"*

This is a man who knew how to nurture the presence of the Lord and the Lord must have enjoyed being in his company greatly as He accepted Abraham's invitation right away. He must have seen how pure Abraham's motive was and did not mind staying for a while. Every time you begin to worship, watch your motives.

As we worship the Lord, corporately or personally, it might be the very day that He has purposed to appear to you in your situation. Your motives determine whether He comes and whether He stays.

Please let a little water be brought

You will notice that right after bowing down, Abraham asked the Lord to allow a little water to be brought so that He may wash His feet. In the Bible days, when a guest visited your house, your first duty as a host was to provide water for the washing of his feet. It was done for hospitality purposes since there were no cars or planes and people had to walk for very long distances and with that came all the dust from the roads. This is why every guest was given some water for their feet. Every other entertainment came after that.

Abraham was very skillful in how he *"detained"* the Lord until His worship turned into *communication*, *fellowship* and then *intercession*. Through offering a sacrifice, He was able to "hold" the Lord until He revealed His plan about destroying Sodom and Gomorrah which began a process of intercession from Abraham.

I grew up on a farm in Kenya and my dad has every domestic animal you might think of. I particularly got drawn to how Abraham ordered a lamb to be slaughtered and prepared for the Lord. Now, if you know anything about slaughtering animals, it's not a ten minute job, and the text above implies that the Lord was ***just passing by and may have been in a hurry*** since He'd planned to go to Sodom and Gomorrah to destroy it. Yet when Abraham offered to entertain Him He stayed! This is the power of worship!

It takes about an hour to slaughter and skin a lamb, clean its guts and another hour or more to roast the meat until it's well done. This tells me that the Lord will make time for a worshiper. He appears to be in a hurry when He shows up but upon your welcome and entertainment to stay longer, He will make time for you to offer your sacrifice of praise and worship to Him, then as you fellowship with Him and as He eats of your "worship", He begins revealing things to you that only come through that kind of intimacy. We see Him pondering, "How can I hide this thing from Abraham!" Because Abraham had done the whole nine yard in entertaining the Lord, the Lord told Him about giving him a son in the coming year and as the communion progressed, he provoked the Lord to share His secrets with him and even allow him to bargain on behalf of the city of Sodom and Gomorrah. If he hadn't made the time to welcome, sacrifice, entertain, fellowship and commune with the Lord, he probably would not have known anything that was about to happen and would have found out about Sodom and Gomorrah being burned in the news like everyone else. But because Abraham recognized a moment of visitation and made up his mind to persist in worship, he was able to save his nephew's life. How many times have we missed on divine secrets because we rushed through a session of worship? How many of us have perished because we had no time to entertain the Lord? We are somehow okay with the Lord showing up but are also afraid He will take up too much time on our tight schedules, so we cut Him off prematurely.

The process of slaughtering and preparing the lamb is also a symbolic of the progression of worship. Some things must die for you to fully worship the Lord in Spirit and in truth. You must be willing to die to the flesh as worshiping Him is through Spirit to spirit only. Flesh cannot understand this. The Lord is willing to make time for your worship and what was supposed to be a visitation could end up becoming a habitation.

It also takes time to worship and it is absolutely impossible to worship the Lord in a hurry. This is why it has to become a lifestyle. It must be our way of living in the present continuous tense. You can't just depend on Sunday morning worship at your local church. The enemy knows this and that's why every day he is erecting new idols in our hearts to distract us from the main thing. Sometimes you will find your attention totally turned to a different direction or on a particular object or person. It is up to you to realize that it is a form of idolatry erected by the enemy to take your eyes off of Jesus. As the old hymn goes,

> *Turn your eyes upon Jesus,*
> *Look full in His wonderful face,*
> *And the things of earth will grow strangely dim,*
> *In the light of His glory and grace.*

When our eyes are off of Jesus, the direct opposite happens – the things of earth get brighter as the glory of God fades from our lives slowly by slowly.

Jesus Himself said it best to Martha when she was complaining about her sister not helping her out in the kitchen in Luke 10:38-42.

"Now it happened as they went that He entered a certain village; and a certain woman named Martha welcomed Him into her house. And she had a sister called Mary, who also sat at Jesus' feet and heard His word. But Martha was distracted with much serving, and she approached Him and said, "Lord, do You not care that my sister has left me to serve alone? Therefore tell her to help me." And Jesus answered and said to her, "Martha, Martha, you are worried and troubled about many things. But one thing is needed, and Mary has chosen that good part, which will not be taken away from her." We will look deeper into this scripture in the chapter on extravagant worship.

CHAPTER FOUR

Extravagant Worship

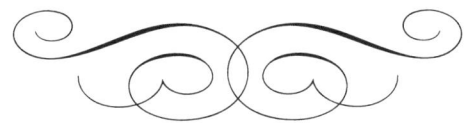

One of my favorite stories on extravagant worship in the Bible is about Mary of Bethany and I believe that we have all been called into this lifestyle. She is described three times in Scripture and I want us to look at her life. Every time she is mentioned, she is at the feet of Jesus. She was able to leave a mark in the heart of Jesus just by doing this. She is not celebrated by the people around her because what is famous with the Lord is not famous with man and what the Lord approves mostly doesn't make it in the books of man. I want to make a mark in God's history book and not just in man's. Let's take a look at her life starting with the one in Luke 10:38-42. *"Now it happened as they went that He entered a certain village; and a certain woman named Martha welcomed Him into her house. And she had a sister called Mary, who also sat at Jesus' feet and heard His word. But Martha was distracted with much serving, and she*

approached Him and said, "Lord, do You not care that my sister has left me to serve alone? Therefore tell her to help me."

And Jesus answered and said to her, "Martha, Martha, you are worried and troubled about many things. But one thing is needed, and Mary has chosen that good part, which will not be taken away from her."

From the passage we see that Mary's custom was to sit at the feet of Jesus and listen to His Word. But Martha was distracted with much serving and she approached Jesus and said, "Lord, do You not care that my sister has left me to serve alone?" Therefore tell her to help me," She literally wanted Jesus to command Mary to get up from His feet and serve. The Bible here says that Martha was distracted with much serving. How can you get distracted with much serving? I thought Jesus said that the servant was greater? It is when we serve in the wrong spirit and want the recognition of man other than the Lord's attention.

The correction to Martha was not that she was in the kitchen while her sister sat at the feet of Jesus. It is a good thing to be in the kitchen and to serve other people. When we don't have someone in the kitchen a lot of things go wrong. She was corrected for doing it in the wrong spirit. In Rev 2:1-5, the Bible says, "To the angel of the church of Ephesus write, 'These things says He who holds the seven stars in His right hand, who walks in the midst of the seven golden lamp stands: "I know your works, your labor, your patience, and that you cannot bear those who are evil. And you have tested those who say they are apostles and are not, and have found them liars; and you have persevered and have patience, and have labored for My name's sake and have not become weary. Nevertheless I have this against you, that you have left your first love. Remember *therefore from where you have fallen; repent and do the first works, or else I will come to you quickly and remove your lampstand from its place— unless you repent.*

Here, Jesus is saying to this church, that He knows they have been working for Him and are doing a lot to please Him. He however has something against them and that is that they do not love Him as they used to. He said He wanted them to repent and to recommit to loving Him again. The members of this church had become workers for God, but they were no longer lovers of God. In as much as we are called to be workers for God, we are to be His lovers first, then workers second. Lovers of God will always outwork workers. They will stay the course through the long haul. The workers get burned out after a while but someone moved by love stays with it for the long haul.

You may be reading this right now and are currently distracted by much serving because you have allowed it to fall into first place and your devotion to the Lord has come to second place and now find yourself critical of others and probably burnt out too. I would encourage you to recommit to the Lord in this moment. Tell Him "*Lord I'm coming back to the heart of worship where it is all about You. I'm sorry for putting the work of the Lord first place and forgetting You the Lord of the work. Thank You for nudging me today to come back to the main thing. Amen.*"

We see that the Lord came to Mary's defense by saying that she had done the good thing. That only one thing was needed and Mary had chosen it. He even went as far as saying that it would not be taken from her. What a powerful statement! It means that one thing is needed as the main thing. All the other things will come into place if this one thing is in place. If you get this one thing in your life, all the other pieces of the puzzle in your life will fall into place. And if this one thing is not in place in your life, you will have a skewed view of all the other issues.

If we study the Word on a regular basis and sit before the Lord, then we will carry the Word in our hearts throughout. You will find that doing this as a worshiper you will revolutionize your life. This is where you will get the language to speak back to the Lord. Forget about all the cute quotes on social media from your favorite people that you keep sharing, when you speak the word of God back to Him in worship, it has power and because His word will not return to Him void, it touches His heart and He fulfils what He said He would do.

Isaiah 55:10-11 says,

"For as the rain comes down, and the snow from heaven,
And do not return there,
But water the earth,
And make it bring forth and bud,
That it may give seed to the sower
And bread to the eater,
So shall My word be that goes forth from My mouth;
It shall not return to Me void,
But it shall accomplish what I please,
And it shall prosper in the thing for which I sent it."

If you abide in the word of the Lord as a worshiper, you will be able to feed others, have a sustained ministry, you will bear fruit, have the ability to walk this walk and not just talk it because I know by now you have realized how much *"worship language"* there is nowadays in the Body of Christ but it is the FRUIT that speaks! You will also have freshness in your spirit all the time and will never wither! How powerful is this?

Read Psalm 1:3,

"He shall be like a tree
Planted by the rivers of water,
That brings forth its fruit in its season,
Whose leaf also shall not wither;
And whatever he does shall prosper."

The Word of God creates a living dialogue in our hearts that we can use to speak back to the Lord in worship. Take time as a worshiper to sit down before the Lord in His word. As you do this, you are also replenishing yourself for the next pour to the Lord. I don't know if you understand this. Let me paint a picture… when you minster to the Lord, you are pouring out from your Spirit and when you eat His word, you are replenishing yourself so that you will have something to pour out next time. I always find that the more I worship the Lord, the more I want to worship Him. I am not bragging but I never get tired of worshiping! I have learnt to keep my tank (Spirit) full of gas (Word) and what that does is create a response in your heart back to the Lord.

The other point I want us to see in this passage is that Mary *"Chose"* that good thing. You have to choose to fill yourself up with the word of God and then and only then can the Holy Spirit move on it. It is a personal choice and no one else can do it for you. It is not a onetime thing on Sunday morning when your pastor shares the Word, but a lifestyle of choosing this over and over. It is not going to happen automatically. You have to consciously go after it. In other words, it is not going to happen automatically or by osmosis. No one can lay hands on you to receive this. It is a choice that has to be made by *you*. Mary prepared her heart by feeding on the Word.

The Holy Spirit loves it when we feed on the Word of God and He also weeps when we are walking around malnourished because we won't make a choice to eat what has been set before us. It is like a newborn baby whose mother's breasts are sour from milk production but the baby won't suck the milk out! It hurts not only the baby but the mother as well because it burns the mother's breasts and the baby gets hurt from hunger and you guessed right, this baby is probably crying all over the place for food! Very sad to even think about it!

The enemy will always come to lead you astray from this place of choosing the Lord and putting Him first all the time. He knows how to keep us distracted. Some have been distracted by an exalted ministry that they have forgotten the simplicity of devotion to the Lord by getting so busy with an exalted ministry. Please always remember that your first ministry is to the Lord and the Holy Spirit will not do for us that which we have been entrusted to do.

The second time we see Mary, it is when her little brother Lazarus dies and she goes to the grave site and falls down, but notice that she is still at the feet of Jesus. She is weeping, but still at His feet and this is no accident. The Holy Spirit is trying to get us to see something. The three times she is mentioned in the Bible, she is always before Him, gazing at His heart, wanting to hear His word.

The third account is right before Jesus was nailed to the cross. Here she is again at His feet, anointing His feet and washing His feet with her hair.

Luke 7:36-50 says, *"Then one of the Pharisees asked Him to eat with him. And He went to the Pharisee's house, and sat down to eat. And behold, a woman in the city who was a sinner, when she knew that Jesus sat at the table in the Pharisee's house, brought an alabaster flask of fragrant oil, and stood at His feet behind Him weeping; and she began to wash His feet with her tears, and wiped them with the hair of her head; and she kissed His feet and anointed them with the fragrant oil. Now when the Pharisee who had invited Him saw this, he spoke to himself, saying, "This Man, if He were a prophet, would know who and what manner of woman this is who is touching Him, for she is a sinner."*

And Jesus answered and said to him, "Simon, I have something to say to you. "So he said, "Teacher, say it." "There was a certain creditor who had two debtors. One owed five hundred denarii, and the other fifty. And when they had nothing with which to repay, he freely forgave them both. Tell Me, therefore, which of them will love him more? "Simon answered and said, "I suppose the one whom he forgave more."

And He said to him, "You have rightly judged." Then He turned to the woman and said to Simon, "Do you see this woman? I entered your house; you gave Me no water for My feet, but she has washed My feet with her tears and wiped them with the hair of her head. You gave Me no kiss, but this woman has not ceased to kiss My feet since the time I came in.

You did not anoint My head with oil, but this woman has anointed My feet with fragrant oil. Therefore I say to you, her sins, which are many, are forgiven, for she loved much. But to whom little is forgiven, the same loves little. "Then He said to her, "Your sins are forgiven. "And those who sat at the table with Him began to say to themselves, "Who is this who even forgives sins? "Then He said to the woman, "Your faith has saved you. Go in peace."

What an audacious extravagant worshiper! She worships Jesus in Holy abandonment in the presence of so much hatred. How do we know there was hatred? A picture is painted for us to make us understand this and that everyone in town knew it. It is quite an uncomfortable place to be in – where everyone knows your business. According to the language used in the Bible, it is implied that she was a prostitute or a woman of ill repute. Therefore it should not come as a surprise to us that in that same room where Jesus was that she had been with several of the men in there, which helps us understand their reaction. But this did not stop her from coming to a party at Simon's house uninvited. One can almost hear the doors fly open and the silence that followed when she walked in and started doing this act of extravagant worship in the presence of all these town people. A woman's hair represents her glory, and, in this moment, she is telling the Lord in her spirit – I lay my glory down for Your glory. The whole house is filled with the fragrance of the perfume. Beloved, if you commit to live this lifestyle before the Lord, you will fill up every room you walk into with the fragrance of Jesus. Your mere presence in a room will affect its spiritual dynamics. Can you imagine now after this extravagant act of worship coming into such a room? I believe that everywhere she went, people could smell the perfume on her and they could also smell it on Jesus even while He was on the cross two days later. Even while they beat Him up, they could still smell it even as it mingled with His blood. Whatever we do in worship will last through eternity because the Lord will remember it as a memorial to you. You see also, it is not one sided. When you pour out your expensive perfume upon Him, He pours it on you too.

Let's look at another version the book of Mark 14:3-9 *says, "And being in Bethany at the house of Simon the leper, as He sat at the table, a woman came having an alabaster flask of very costly oil of spikenard. Then she broke the flask and poured it on His head. But there were some who were indignant among themselves, and said, "Why was this fragrant oil wasted? For it might have been sold for more than three hundred denarii and given to the poor." And they criticized her sharply. But Jesus said, "Let her alone. Why do you trouble her? She has done a good work for Me. For you have the poor with you always, and whenever you wish you may do them good; but Me you do not have always. She has done what she could. She has come beforehand to anoint My body for burial. Assuredly, I say to you, wherever this gospel is preached in the whole world, what this woman has done will also be told as a memorial to her."*

She breaks the jar of perfume and pours it over His head. Worshiping in abandonment requires some dangerous audacity. Can you imagine walking into a room full of haters and going straight to Jesus, breaking down a jar of perfume and pouring it on His head? What an uproar this must have caused! No wonder even the disciples were criticizing her and not only called her a sinner but called the big act a waste. When you see Jesus nothing else matters! There were probably men in this room who had touched her body before; men who *wanted* her but did not really want *her* but Jesus had touched her soul and Spirit. No one looked at her the way Jesus did. He saw her. The real her! He saw the inner beauty that was crying to be released.

You will be criticized sharply in you decide to take on this lifestyle of worship but I want you to understand that the Lord delights in this kind of lifestyle and He calls it "*good*". What they were using to criticize her was such a good thing- for the poor and I want you to know that this will be the typical response of "religious" people when they see an act of genuine spiritual devotion. It is incomprehensible to them and will always be seen as a waste of money, time, opportunity etc. But again, Jesus comes to her defense and now we know her because she had the audacity to ignore her fears and worship Jesus.

Extravagant worship always wins out with God over pious garb. He looks at the heart and welcomes the open unfeigned adoration of His children however it is expressed and, this is why Jesus jealously rose to her defense cutting through their pious hypocrisy right to their hearts. Jesus said in Matthew 6:21 that wherever a man's treasure is, that is where the heart will be also. In this case, Mary's heart was in the right place and Jesus affirmed her. She wasted everything she had ever earned on Him!

There is another very important principle that I want you to get in this passage; that she broke the jar of perfume. Most of the times when we buy perfume, it comes with an atomizer at the top of the bottle so that the scent is kept intact and to also prevent it from just pouring out. You and I are the vessels that carry this expensive perfume of worship before the Lord but to be able to do it in the abandonment displayed by

Mary; we have to be broken before the Lord such that we lose the control we have over our worship. Some of us have wonderful control and do not want anyone to see our emotions as we worship but this should not be the case. Stop trying to control every aspect of your worship. Lose all that wonderful control and allow the Holy Spirit to take over and you will end up releasing the fragrance of Jesus in your entire church and region.

Brokenness happens to us through the things that the Lord allows to happen to us on our journey in life. If you learn to allow the Lord to form you into the vessel He desires to see in you even though what you go through might be painful, you will carry this fragrance of worship within you. People will not be able to put their hand on what it is about you that is different when you worship.

I'd like to teach you something powerful I learned about brokenness and how it releases the fragrance within. Brokenness is not about emotionalism. It is an act of the will to surrender our will to God's will. To say yes to what God wants over what you want. It is acknowledging your need for Him. It is here that God strips you of your self-sufficiency by stripping you of your pride. Nothing can be used to better describe the picture of brokenness than a wild stallion that still wants its independence. The process of breaking it is a rigorous one where a cowboy gets on its back and rides it. It however does not want to be ridden and so it keeps bucking and tries to throw the cowboy off its back and sometimes he gets thrown off by the stallion but if the goal is to break him, he rides him till he gets broken and the only way to know that it has been broken is that it is now under someone else's control. It does what the owner wants it to do and allows the owner to ride it. It is the same with us. When it is time for God to break us, He gets hold the crevices of our pride, independence and sin so that we are transparent in Spirit before Him such that even when we worship Him, we lose all the control we previously possessed. When you are broken before Him, you allow Him to ride you and by this I mean use you as a vessel for His glory. You do not have time to be cute when it is time to worship and praise Him. Sure enough you might try to get hold of yourself but the fragrance within you cannot be contained any more since your jar of perfume has been broken.

John 12:24 *Most assuredly, I say to you, unless a grain of wheat falls to the ground and dies, it remains alone; but if it dies, it produces much grain.*

Inside every seed is a greater life than you can see. When you look at a seed all you see is the outer (exterior) shell but life is in the seed but it will only come to life when death occurs to the outer shell first. When that seed is buried and the shell is broken, all the life that is held within is released. Death is necessary for life and in this case, death to the flesh. Psalm 34:18 *The Lord is near to those who have a broken heart, and saves such as have a contrite spirit.*

When somebody joins the army, the sergeant breaks them. You can no longer do what you were accustomed to doing as a civilian and the more you rebel, he stays on you till he breaks you. Your answer will only be "Yes Sir!" or "Yes Ma'am!" He has to strip you of all you brought in order to remake you into what he wants you to be. Everyone that God has used greatly, He had to break greatly. Do you want to be used greatly by the Lord in worship? Then you must surrender to a greater level of breaking. It is better to surrender to be broken by the Lord instead of fighting it. Say to the Lord right now, *"Lord, break me! I give You the right to strip me off of all my independence and everything in me that is not like You. I am scared, but I am just going to trust that You love me enough to know what I can handle."* Amen.

Or you can run like the wild stallion described above and He will have to break you without your permission. It takes a lot longer for this one and you have to go through much more. Brokenness keeps you humble. It doesn't matter what accolades they put on your name, you know the Name that is higher!

In conclusion, worshipers, let us create a sustained lifestyle of cultivating a heart that is responsive to God, be zealous with the zeal of God and pour out our all at His feet in brokenness.

CHAPTER 5

What Happens When We Worship?

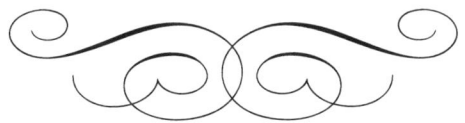

These are just some of the things that happen to us when we worship. As you go through the different chapters of the book, you will learn more of what happens when we enthrone the Lord.

One of the first things that happens when we worship is that _**we are changed from the inside out**_ because when you see God for who He really is as Isaiah did, you start to see yourself. The real you! When you see His beauty and holiness in worship, it causes you to closely examine yourself and the things that you do. Suddenly you want to change your ways so that you can be like Him. You can't tell me you're a worshiper and you haven't changed one bit! Seeing God's holiness and beauty so closely -because He does come when we worship in Spirit and in Truth, will cause you to turn your life around! You see the trash that is in your heart and life that didn't bother you before and you make up your mind to change so that you can accommodate the Lord more. Genuine worship will always lead to personal examination. You will see His worth and will desire to give Him your best because He is holy. It is saying "*I esteem You very highly so I will adjust my life accordingly so that you can inhabit my life.*"

In Isaiah 6:1-6 *So I said: "Woe is me, for I am undone! Because I am a man of unclean lips, and I dwell in the midst of a people of unclean lips; for my eyes have seen the King, the Lord of hosts." The one of the seraphim flew to me, having in his hand a live coal which he had taken with the tongs from the altar, and he touched my mouth with it and said: "Behold this has touched your lips; your iniquity is taken away and your sin is purged."*

When Isaiah came in contact with the glory of God, he recognized his weakness, acknowledged that he had an issue and then he allowed the Lord to sanitize and purge that area of his life so that he could be used of the Lord. His mouth was burned with a burning coal of fire. Can you see how wicked the enemy is? He knew that Isaiah's mouth was what the Lord had purposed to use in his ministry to declare what thus says the Lord so he had set Isaiah up in using his mouth for something that would constantly defile him and make him ineffective. He allowed him to have a certain degree of it as we can see he had prophesied in the previous five chapters but not as powerfully as he did after getting that weakness taken care of in the presence of the Lord. And how he would have missed his destiny! He ended up becoming one of the greatest prophets mostly referred to as the eagle prophet. Notice that the fire of the Lord touched him at the exact point of his confession "*I am a man of unclean lips*" His lips were turned into anointed lips to speak the Word of the Lord. The lips are a very sensitive part of the body. Can you imagine the pain of having them seared with a red hot coal! When you come into the presence of the Lord in worship, what area do you feel that you need to work on? Will you allow Him to purge that area? Are you willing to work with the Lord? Because worship of a holy God demands that you change your fleshly tendencies. Please pause and think about this.

Another thing that happens when **_we worship is that the Lord tells us who we are in Him and even reveals our destinies to us._** It is absolutely impossible to spend an hour telling the Lord who He is and He not tell you who you are. He is not an unjust God! I was only a teenager and I was sitting outside our house in the dark watching the stars as I sung to the Lord. I didn't have any microphone so I used to enjoy how the sound traveled far in the night. A lot of stuff had happened in my life and I couldn't talk to anyone about it, so my way of escape was outside every evening singing to the Lord. I had never heard His voice before but this one night as I worshiped Him, He told me about what would happen to my family in the future and also how he would raise me up in the Kingdom to serve Him. He was a very relatable God to me even at that age unlike the angry God who had been portrayed in most teachings that I had heard in church those days. He laughed a lot just like my dad. So I was never scared to tell Him who He was to me in my own little language. I used to sing to Him mostly and write Him letters.

The more I told Him who He was, the more He told me who I was. I had never been prophesied to by anyone and I didn't care to seek prophecies because in the presence of the Lord, He told me exactly who I was and what I would do. I knew I was called to preach because He would show me myself in auditoriums preaching just like my dad. I knew I was going to America because He told me as I worshiped. Etc. what I'm trying to get across here is that He tells you who you are as you worship Him. He also reveals mysteries to you as we saw in the case of Abraham detaining the Lord. Secrets that others don't know, He tells you!

Another thing that happens when we worship is that, **_when you worship, God releases stuff that was tied up_**. We see this in Abraham's case right after his act of worship before the Lord Genesis 22:11-14. "*But the Angel of the Lord called to him from heaven and said, "Abraham, Abraham!" So he said, "Here I am."And He said, "Do not lay your hand on the lad, or do anything to him; for now I know that you fear God, since you have not withheld your son, your only son, from Me." Then Abraham lifted his eyes and looked, and there behind him was a ram caught in a thicket by its horns. So Abraham went and took the ram, and offered it up fora burnt offering instead of his son. And Abraham called the name of the place, The-Lord-Will-Provide; as it is said to this day, "In the Mount of the Lord it shall be provided."*"

Since the Lord is looking to and fro for those who are loyal to Him so that He can show Himself strong on their behalf, when He finds a worshiper, He just gets into show off mode. He will pull heaven and earth to make sure they are not wanting for anything. He will go out of His way to make sure He becomes to you what you are calling Him. Just like a man likes to live up to praise he is given. The Lord has done some very crazy things in my life such that when I'm sharing them with the people that know me; it always looks like I'm telling a type of fiction story but it isn't! When they are trying to understand logically how that could happen to someone when there is a law that blocks it all I know is that Jesus did it! I didn't have to do any funny business; He went in and did the funny business for me! Because when you worship you transcend normal limits. Things that did not belong to you now become part of your possession. You will not even have to fight for some things in your life. Because of how important a worshiper is to the Lord, He will fulfill His end as you continue to minister to Him. He will take the fight off of the ram and all you have to do is retrieve it. You never leave His presence the same way you came in.

I want us to look at a scripture in Matthew 4:1-11 which says, "Then Jesus was led up by the Spirit into the wilderness to be tempted by the devil. And when He had fasted forty days and forty nights, afterward He was hungry. Now when the tempter came to Him, he said, "If You are the Son of God, command that these stones become bread." But He answered and said, "It is written, 'Man shall not live by bread alone, but by every word that proceeds from the mouth of God.' "Then the devil took Him up into the holy city, set Him on the pinnacle of the temple, and said to Him, "If You are the Son of God, throw Yourself down. For it is written: 'He shall give His angels charge over you 'and, 'In their hands they shall bear you up, lest you dash your foot against a stone.' "Jesus said to him, "It is written again, 'You shall not tempt the Lord your God.'" Again, the devil took Him up on an exceedingly high mountain, and showed Him all the kingdoms of the world and their glory. And he said to Him, "All these things I will give You if You will fall down and worship me." Then Jesus said to him, "Away with you, Satan! For it is written, 'You shall worship the Lord your God, and Him only you shall serve.' "Then the devil left Him, and behold, angels came and ministered to Him."

This is right after Jesus was baptized and the Holy Spirit led Him into the wilderness to be tested of the devil. *And he said to Him, "All these things I will give You if You will fall down and worship me." Then Jesus said to him, "Away with you, Satan! For it is written, 'You shall worship the Lord your God, and Him only you shall serve.'* The devil was offering Jesus something on the condition of worship. If the devil can give you kingdoms of this world when you worship him, how *much more* our Father in heaven? The other verse in the same scripture I want us to look at is *then the devil left Him, and behold, angels came and ministered to Him.*

<u>The best way to get rid of the devil is through worship</u>. If he doesn't leave, you haven't worshiped. The moment Jesus redirected the worship to God, satan left Him alone.

<u>While we are worshiping, angels are being released on assignment in our lives.</u> Never underestimate the power of worship. Though your natural eye may not see into the spiritual realm, there's a lot of angelic activity during worship. All for you worshiper! Because you have chosen to set your gaze upon the Lord.

Also, **<u>when we worship the Lord with all of our hearts, it rises up to Him like pure incense and He will move and free all those around us, not leaving our families behind either.</u>** As we worship Him, he is working on us as individuals, our families and those around us get the benefit as well.

Remember the story of Paul and Silas when they were in the prison.

Acts 16:16-34

"Now it happened, as we went to prayer, that a certain slave girl possessed with a spirit of divination met us, who brought her masters much profit by fortune-telling. This girl followed Paul and us, and cried out, saying, "These men are the servants of the Most High God, who proclaim to us the way of salvation." And this she did for many days. But Paul, greatly annoyed, turned and said to the spirit, "I command you in the name of Jesus Christ to come out of her." And he came out that very hour. But when her masters saw that their hope of profit was gone, they seized Paul and Silas and dragged them into the marketplace to the authorities. And they brought them to the magistrates, and said, "These men, being Jews, exceedingly trouble our city; and they teach customs which are not lawful for us, being Romans, to receive or observe. "Then the multitude rose up together against them; and the magistrates tore off their clothes and commanded them to be beaten with rods. And when they had laid many stripes on them, they threw them into prison, commanding the jailer to keep them securely. Having received such a charge, he put them into the inner prison and fastened their feet in the stocks. But at midnight Paul and Silas were praying and singing hymns to God, and the prisoners were listening to them. Suddenly there was a great earthquake, so that the foundations of the prison were shaken; and immediately all the doors were opened and everyone's chains were loosed. And the keeper of the prison, awaking from sleep and seeing the prison doors open, supposing the prisoners had fled, drew his sword and was about to kill himself. But Paul called with a loud voice, saying, "Do yourself no harm, for we are all here." Then he called for a light, ran in, and fell down trembling before Paul and Silas. And he brought them out and said, "Sirs, what must I do to be saved? "So they said, "Believe on the Lord Jesus Christ, and you will be saved, you and your household." Then they spoke the word of the

Lord to him and to all who were in his house. And he took them the same hour of the night and washed their stripes. And immediately he and all his family were baptized. Now when he had brought them into his house, he set food before them; and he rejoiced, having believed in God with all his household."

Every time we offer the Lord our praise and worship wholeheartedly, it not only frees us, but those connected to us as well. Paul and Silas had a very good excuse not to praise or worship God in that moment because after all, He didn't save them from a beating and they were out there doing His work. They should have sat in there like everyone else and cry as they thought about their fate the next morning but instead of that, they offered Him a sacrifice of praise. A sacrifice because their circumstances dictated otherwise. But they chose to praise. The jail breaking was the Lord stepping in into Paul and Silas's praise because He inhabits the praise of His people. The jail conditions here are very different from an austere comfort of an American jail. The inner prisons of the Bible were like a dungeon similar to the one Jeremiah was in. They were contagious cells, damp and cold, from which light was excluded and where the chains rusted on the limbs of the prisoners. We also know that in these prisons, most of the times the prisoners are not allowed to get out to use the bathroom and so they have to do it right there as far as the chains allow them to go. These guys had been beaten with rods and many stripes had been laid upon them. So from the picture painted above, we now understand that they were bleeding and in pain and being put in such conditions didn't help either, but they chose to rejoice that they were counted worthy to suffer for the name of Christ. I can imagine that as time went by the more they bled and got numb from the beating and the worse the smell in the inner prison got. But around midnight when it was getting worse, a sound was heard. It was Paul who led saying *"for the Lord is good and His mercies endure forever*! "And then Silas echoed the same thing. Imagine in a prison filled with prisoners awaiting their fate to be determined by man and then some guys start praising the Lord. Pretty strange isn't it? The normal thing would have been to sit there and wail or in our world today, get a message out to our followers on social media of our last words before the execution. So this explains why the other prisoners did not join in the hymns but were just listening to them. When suddenly as if in direct response to their praise, an earthquake shook the very foundations of that prison, the gates were broken, the bars smitten asunder and the hands of the prisoners loosed. God had broken into the prison! This is the power of our praise and worship. It invites God into our situation and He comes to set His children free.

It is also important to note that sometimes people don't join in worship because they are weighed down and chained by different things in their lives but when we who worship with the revelation of *WHO* God is no matter what we are going through, they eventually get free because of our worship.

CHAPTER 6

Worship Team Leaders

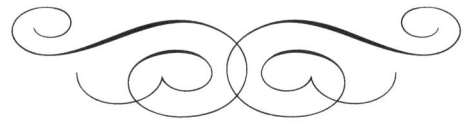

On this chapter, we are going to focus mainly on those of us who lead a team in a church or ministry. When you're working with less than you should have - this includes equipment, gifts or the entire team, be faithful in that phase and polish your gift as you trust the Lord to increase your arsenal one day. When David was in the fields with his father's sheep, all he had was a sling and the stones he used to protect his father's sheep. I can imagine him wishing he had a sword or another weapon like the other boys in his neighborhood but since he did not have these, he had to have been spending lots of hours in a day practicing how to protect his sheep by hitting imaginary targets using his sling and stone until he mastered how to hit a certain spot each day so that on the day he finally met Goliath, he killed him with that which many would have considered less equipment – a sling, and then also graduated to using a sword in that very moment. When the bible describes Goliath's sword when David was seeking a weapon as he fled from Saul, and the man of God told him that only this was available, David said that there was that there was none like it. 1 Samuel 21:9 *"So the priest said, "The sword of Goliath the Philistine, whom you killed in the Valley of Elah, there it is, wrapped in a cloth behind the ephod. If you will take that, take it. For there is no other except that one here." And David said, "There is none like it; give it to me."*

It seems to me that David knew how to maximize the little the Lord made available to him because this is the same man who turned a group of disgruntled team of men into Israel's mightiest men of war from the cave of adullam to the battlefield. 1 Samuel 22:1-2 *"David therefore departed from there and escaped to the cave of Adullam. So when his brothers and all his father's house heard it, they went down there to him. 2 And everyone who was in distress, everyone who was in debt, and everyone who was discontented gathered to him. So he became captain over them. And there were about four hundred men with him."*

Imagine getting such a large group of people that even the Bible describes them as distressed and disgruntled. This goes to show you as a leader that you are not getting that *"perfect"* group of people you've been waiting on. The people that the Lord has given to you have the potential to be the best team you ever had even though they seem rough around the edges right now. It is you who will turn them into the perfect team. You have been handpicked by the Lord and equipped to turn them into a team of mighty men and women of war. They came to David as a worthless team and the next time they're mentioned in the Bible in 2

Samuel 23:8-38, those that stuck it out with David are honored as Israel's mightiest warriors. Hallelujah!

"These are the names of the mighty men whom David had: Josheb-Basshebeth the Tachmonite, chief among the captains. He was called Adino the Eznite, because he had killed eight hundred men at one time. And after him was Eleazar the son of Dodo, the Ahohite, one of the three mighty men with David when they defied the Philistines who were gathered there for battle, and the men of Israel had retreated. He arose and attacked the Philistines until his hand was weary, and his hand stuck to the sword. The Lord brought about a great victory that day; and the people returned after him only to plunder. And after him was Shammah the son of Agee the Hararite. The Philistines had gathered together into a troop where there was a piece of ground full of lentils. So the people fled from the Philistines. But he stationed himself in the middle of the field, defended it, and killed the Philistines. So the Lord brought about a great victory. Then three of the thirty chief men went down at harvest time and came to David at the cave of Adullam. And the troop of Philistines encamped in the Valley of Rephaim. David was then in the stronghold, and the garrison of the Philistines was then in Bethlehem. And David said with longing, "Oh, that someone would give me a drink of the water from the well of Bethlehem, which is by the gate!" So the three mighty men broke through the camp of the Philistines, drew water from the well of Bethlehem that was by the gate, and took it and brought it to David. Nevertheless he would not drink it, but poured it out to the Lord. And he said, "Far be it from me, O Lord, that I should do this! Is this not the blood of the men who went in jeopardy of their lives?" Therefore he would not drink it. These things were done by the three mighty men. Now Abishai the

brother of Joab, the son of Zeruiah, was chief of another three. He lifted his spear against three hundred men, killed them, and won a name among these three. Was he not the most honored of three? Therefore he became their captain. However, he did not attain to the first three. Benaiah was the son of Jehoiada, the son of a valiant man from Kabzeel, who had done many deeds. He had killed two lion-like heroes of Moab. He also had gone down and killed a lion in the midst of a pit on a snowy day. And he killed an Egyptian, a spectacular man. The Egyptian had a spear in his hand; so he went down to him with a staff, wrested the spear out of the Egyptian's hand, and killed him with his own spear. These things Benaiah the son of Jehoiada did, and won a name among three mighty men. He was more honored than the thirty, but he did not attain to the first three. And David appointed him over his guard. Asahel the brother of Joab was one of the thirty; Elhanan the son of Dodo of Bethlehem, Shammah the Harodite, Elika the Harodite, Helez the Paltite, Ira the son of Ikkesh the Tekoite, Abiezer the Anathothite, Mebunnai the Hushathite, Zalmon the Ahohite, Maharai the Netophathite, Heleb the son of Baanah (the Netophathite), Ittai the son of Ribai from Gibeah of the children of Benjamin, Benaiah a Pirathonite, Hiddai from the brooks of Gaash, Abi-Albon the Arbathite, Azmaveth the Barhumite, Eliahba the Shaalbonite (of the sons of Jashen), Jonathan, Shammah the Hararite, Ahiam the son of Sharar the Hararite, Eliphelet the son of Ahasbai, the son of the Maachathite, Eliam the son of Ahithophel the Gilonite, Hezrai the Carmelite, Paarai the Arbite, Igal the son of Nathan of Zobah, Bani the Gadite, Zelek the Ammonite, Naharai the Beerothite (armorbearer of Joab the son of Zeruiah), Ira the Ithrite, Gareb the Ithrite, and Uriah the Hittite: thirty-seven in all."

What would you say are the less than perfect conditions/equipment the Lord has you working with in this season? I remember during my leadership tenure with a certain worship team, I didn't have a keyboard player and for a long time I led without one. You see when I was growing up; all I used was a drum so I had led praise and worship without most instruments for quite some time and so this didn't faze me. The presence of the Lord is not dependent on what instruments are being played, although this does help us as worship leaders.

I mastered how to entertain the Lord under these circumstances that most would have considered unfavorable. I would go home extremely worn out especially because this was back in Kenya and because of sometimes not even having a microphone we had to project our voices over the congregation so it really took a lot out of us. I did it passionately every Sunday not knowing that I was in training.

The presence of the Lord would manifest and sometimes we would end up in prayer or praise and worship all day or night. Eventually we ended up getting a keyboard and guitar and supernaturally one of our team members learnt how to play it within no time and now I had to learn how to lead with instruments.

So, fast forward to 2009 now in the United States, I continued leading as I trusted and prayed that we would get musicians in our team one day. When I finally got a keyboard player, he didn't come as a keyboard player at first. He came to me with a guitar and he could only play a few chords but he was willing. I saw the potential in him and nurtured him through love and encouragement until today; he is one of the best keyboard players I have ministered with, very learned in the prophetic sound.

You see as a team leader, the people that the Lord has given you are not for you to lord over but to love as you believe in them before they even believe in themselves. People tend to believe that they can do anything if the person leading them believes in them too, and trust me; each person that the Lord has sent to you has exactly what you need in your team! If you are keen and prayerful about them, you will see areas of gifting in them that they had no idea about and you as a leader have been entrusted to pull it out through nurturing. If only we as leaders would nurture, like a mother the different gifts that have been sent to us! Just because you are leading a team doesn't mean that you are better than them. In fact, it is you that the Lord wants to work on while you're leading the different personalities. You might be having the title of *leader* but in your team could be some very high ranking people in the Spirit. So, be respectful and mindful of this at all times. Watch your tone and be sensitive to the ones under your leadership. You don't always have to have the last say in the team. Allow your team members to be and also express themselves. Don't be a bully! You will give an account before the Lord.

It is also equally important that the people who are being led honor their team leaders. Sure enough you might be more learned than them or can even sing better than them, but the Lord has appointed them to lead you so have honor and respect towards them. Romans 13:7 says, *"Render therefore to all their due: taxes to whom taxes are due, customs to whom customs, fear to whom fear, honor to whom honor."* I always used this illustration in my team. I would ask the team to think about us all lined up on the altar by responsibility and then to imagine that someone had broken into the church and had started fighting. Would they run to the back to fight or would they attack the person at the very front? And we would all talk and agree that it is the leader who would be first to get attacked and the others would probably have enough time to run or hide. So being a leader is a position in the battlefront and the arrows hit them first before they hit everyone else. It is a position that requires a lot of responsibility and sacrifice. So honor your leaders. Be kind to them. They will make mistakes too but be gracious with them. Love on them! Some of these leaders are very lonely people because often time people don't want to associate themselves with them.

In the same team that I was leading, there were people who could not sing. Well I know the question you're about to ask me right now, "Shiro, now why would you have someone in the worship team that can't sing?" And this is a valid question so I'm going to answer it as we move along. The people who could not sing as well as the others were worshipers too. Singing has nothing to do with being a worshiper as we established earlier. Being a worshiper is more about the posture of the heart before the Lord. It is your duty as a worship team leader to know *why you have certain persons in your team*. This will prevent overlooking them while putting the others on a pedestal. You see, I had some people who could sing their faces off in my team and others who could not sing who were there specifically for the worship team but for a different purpose like prayer, the prophetic etc. We were well equipped for every need that would arise. When it came time to singing, I knew who to give the microphone but when I needed something shifted in the atmosphere, I also knew who to call upon. This created balance amongst us, and no one felt overlooked or useless to the team neither did we have any kind of entitlement amongst us.

Also, it is very important for the worship team to fast and pray together. This helps in bringing all spirits of the team members in subjection to the Holy Spirit. In this team, we fasted every Friday and Sunday morning until the service was over. The only person I allowed to eat breakfast on Sunday was the drummer because he was very young when he came to me and he had to do a great deal of beating the drum during the services and it would wear him out although overtime he was able to do it as he grew older. We did unity intercession prayer on Friday night before rehearsal and then on Sunday mornings for about an hour before getting on the altar to start going over what we had practiced on Friday night. Now, you might do it differently at your church, just make sure you pray together. I love excellence and want each one of us to sound good, but my main emphasis has been on entertaining the presence of the Lord. Teach your team members how to host the presence of the Lord. No amount of vocal ability or singing will ever replace the presence! I am more interested in the Lord showing up than us tickling the ears of man with our *oohhs and ahhs*. Now, I do not mean that we don't perfect our gifts, but even as we perfect our gifts, let's also perfect entertaining the presence of the Lord. You see, if you or I don't show up for service on Sunday, it will not be a big deal because we have never saved or healed anyone. but there will be a big problem if the One we are worshiping does not show up!

This is a missing ingredient in most worship teams. You can almost feel the discomfort that sweeps in when this is brought up because we know that when His presence manifests it demands change in certain areas of our lives that we are not yet ready to part with. So we would rather have just a level of it. It is just like the children of Israel who wanted to get close to God but after seeing what it took they told Moses to speak with them instead of God. Exodus 20:18-19 says, "*Now all the people witnessed the thundering, the lightning flashes, the sound of the trumpet, and the mountain smoking ;and when the people saw it, they trembled and stood afar off. Then they said to Moses, "You speak with us, and we will hear; but let not God speak with us, lest we die."* When you say that you are ready for the Lord to show up in your worship do you mean it or is this just another one of your worship languages? Do you really want Him? Do you know how to entertain Him if He comes? The presence of God has to be so important to you such that like Moses, you refuse to move until He shows up.

I used to have this lady in my team who could not sing. She was mostly in prayer in the team and I would call on her sometimes to help me shift the atmosphere during service. She would lead the prayer and we would go on but sometimes she would start singing and she mostly led "*You are great, You do miracles so great*" Judging by her vocal ability, she would have failed miserably but she was doing something so crazy in the realm of the Spirit with her bad voice and all. Because worship is not about how good you can sing! Song is just one of the expressions of worship.

There were also other gifts in the team especially in the prophetic and with all these different types of people that the Lord had given to my leadership; I had to rely on Him to help me how to know what they carried and how to deal with each one of them effectively. Sometimes it was very overwhelming as we know how it is in most worship teams- clashing of personalities from different backgrounds and it is upon you as the team leader to purge some of this stuff out of the team for the good of the church as a whole. Several individuals would join thinking it was all about glitz and glamour under the lights only to find out the high price that the altar demands, it wasn't long before they dropped out. It took the grace of God to lead this team and as we grew together, I was very proud to see how each one's gift progressively manifested on the altar.

We practiced for hours not just as a rehearsal but as though we were in the main service. We learnt how to nurture the presence of the Lord. During our practice sessions the presence of God would manifest Himself and we would end up staying throughout the night in worship and then when we met on Sunday morning, what happened on Friday night during rehearsal would repeat during the service. The Lord would show up in the services and the programmer couldn't program or the preacher able to preach. In this atmosphere, all sorts of miracles would happen. We were ruined for His glory and so this created such a hunger and thirst for the Lord in everyone, the congregation included! We all showed up with an expectation for His glory. Just because it is rehearsal time does not mean that you kick the Holy Spirit out. I heard some-one say once that they were tired of hearing about the Holy Spirit and anointing during practice because they wanted their team to work on perfecting their skill. You see, you will not be able to perfect your skill to sing or play without the Holy Spirit. He is our Helper and He helps in rehearsal too. If you kick Him out during rehearsal but then when you get on the altar then start telling Him how much you need Him to come and help you, do you think He will come? You disrespected Him earlier! The Holy Spirit is a Person and we should be very mindful of how we speak to and of Him. There is also the other extreme group of people who refuse to practice because they say that they are depending on the Holy Spirit. The Holy Spirit is not the author of confusion. He will not be part of confusion and disorder. He breathes upon what we have prepared faithfully in His presence. Frustration will be the portion of those who do not prepare and then expect Him to come.

Practice what you have in your hand faithfully and the Lord will breathe on it. Like I mentioned earlier, David only had two things mastered in the secret place which got him to the palace. He had mastered his skill on the harp and his aim on the slingshot. These seemingly unimportant things became just the thing that he needed to fulfill his destiny. Do your part effectively and let the Lord do His part. He will not do for you what He has anointed you to do. Do your part and then supernatural will kick in.

As the Lord has poured into you as a worship leader and entrusted you to lead a group of people, He wants you to also mentor other people not just through your lifestyle but by teaching them what you know. Hoarding information and other things that can make your worship team better is not good because as a worship team leader, you are also a pastor. You have a responsibility of shepherding those you are leading. The people you have now in your team are the ones the Lord has sent you in this season to train and love. I know you want the people you lead to "*get it*" like you do but often times what comes out of you as *fruit* will be *seed* to the ones receiving it. Be patient and allow them to grow. Love the people God has sent to you and make them feel valuable to the team.

As a matter of fact, if you hoard information and refuse to release it to others you also get stagnant. It is when you release information that the river within you continues to flow with freshness because the Lord releases more to you as He can see that you are being a good steward of the information through teaching others.

There also has to be a ***marriage between the worship leader and the pastor***. Now I do not mean that you literally marry your pastor if you are a worship leader but I am talking about being in unity with your pastor (*now, if you are a worship leader married to your pastor good!*). You have to understand that you and your pastor are on the same page. You are not there to fight your pastor because according to you, you think that you ought to have fifteen more minutes of worship and he won't allow you to have it. So one of your key points in prayer is to rebuke the spirit of resistance to worship in your pastor and you have been very diligent with it. On the other hand, pastors want more time to preach. Oh I've been in church forever so I know this game. It would be wise to step down if you are a worship leader who is not on the same page with the church pastor otherwise this will cause a lot of division in the church since you are spreading your own agenda than what the pastor is trying to do. You are serving in that church because of the vision the Lord gave your pastor and it is not wise to go in with your own private agenda.

There is only room for one vision in a church; anything else is di-vision. Have a good understanding of the pastor's vision for the church and commit and submit to it. Psalm 133:1-2 says, *"Behold, how good and how pleasant it is for brethren to dwell together in unity! It (unity) is like the precious ointment (anointing) upon the head that ran down upon the beard even Aaron's beard: that went down to the skirts of his garments.*" The anointing that is on the head will eventually flow to all the other parts of the body.

It is very important for worship leaders ***to submit to the authority of God and then submit to the authority of the leadership that they are under***. This way, the enemy has no breach to come in through because he can sense a spirit of rebellion which the Bible says is as the same as witchcraft. Stay in communication with your pastor! If you have a suggestion, always go directly to you pastor. Do not allow the enemy to contaminate your heart through unnecessary talk or gossip about your pastor. Sometimes the enemy will place people strategically on your path to discredit the man or woman of God you have been sent to serve under. If you do not close this door, you will not be able to serve effectively because your heart will be swayed.

Talk to your pastor, ask questions on what their expectation of you as a worship leader is and try to implement that into your team. Stop taking suggestions and compliments from the congregation- although some of them are good and can be implemented, always run them by your pastor. Sometimes worship leaders' ears get very itchy and they want to get compliments about a session they led so they go fishing in the congregation and the enemy can use this to plant a seed in you. The only compliments you want to hear, of whether you are doing a good job or not should be coming from God and your pastor because you are there to serve the Lord and your pastor. (This doesn't also mean that you go fishing for them). You are there to help your pastor in this area.

After each worship session, I like to evaluate myself even before I check with my pastor. I usually ask the Holy Spirit to show me where

I could have done better or why a certain thing happened during the service. Then I ask Him to teach me how to go about it next time. When you avail yourself to His guidance and teaching, even as you lead on the altar He will still be guiding you. It happens all the time when I'm leading, I tell Him that *"I have availed my ear to You. Tell me whatever You want me to do. This is not my service but Your service Lord, lead me in the direction You want us to go in today. I know I have prepared this, but I allow You to frustrate my agenda today!"* and because He is our precious Holy Spirit, He does it. He will guide you too if you take hard hearing out of yourself and not just pretending to be submissive to Him when you mount the altar. He knows when you are flattering Him. Psalm 32:8-9 says, *"I will instruct you and teach you in the way you should go; I will counsel you (who are willing to learn) I will guide you with My eye. Do not be like the horse or like the mule which have no understanding, which must be harnessed with bit and bridle else they will not come near you."*

Also, __*be alert in the Spirit for change of seasons*__. This will help you in choosing of the songs you should lead. When you sense that the seasons have changed in the Spirit, always check with your pastor to see what direction he feels you should take. There was this video that was floating online a while back. The pastor seemed to have finished preaching a very serious message and he asked the worship team to lead a song not specifying which particular song. In such a moment, he was counting on the worship leader to pick a song in line with his sermon that morning. The worship leader started a song and the pastor had stopped her so abruptly and rebuked her sharply about the song that had been led and the church not wanting to hear that same song again because they had been singing it for a while. The congregation can be heard in the video reacting to this too as though affirming what the pastor had said. You see, there was nothing wrong with the song she led, it was actually a powerful song on encouragement but because the worship leader did not discern the change of season, that's why it was wrong in that context. It was very embarrassing to even watch. I felt bad for them.

The bible says in 1 Chronicles 12:32 says, "*The sons of Issachar were men that had the understanding of the times, and knew what Israel had to do.*" As a worship leader, it is upon you to seek the Lord and know what season you are in as an individual and also the season of the church. If you are unsure, always speak to your pastor about this. You noticed I added your season as an individual in the last sentence. Yes, your season because you might be going through your own stuff for example mourning, but the church is not mourning at that particular time. So if you do not differentiate the two and keep them separate, you might usher the church into a mourning season when they are supposed to be rejoicing.

I had this lady that was in my worship team and she always loved to get us into warfare every time she led. She would scream at us and command us to fight especially the worship team and the congregation would join in the fight but it seemed the more we screamed the harder the atmosphere got because the church was actually in a rejoicing season that demanded more praise and thanksgiving after we had achieved a major victory and the Lord had finally given us rest. This went on each time she was appointed to lead until one day I had to step in and talk to all my team members about it and the sigh of relief from some of them was very telling. I later came to find out that it was a personal battle that she had going on privately and I used that moment to teach her about the personal and corporate seasons. Another one of my worship leaders would keep us in the rain season and I had to teach too that we only ask for rain *in the time of rain* which simply means the season of rain. Zechariah 10:1 says, *"Ask the Lord for rain in the time of the latter rain. The Lord will make flashing clouds; He will give them showers of rain, grass in the field for everyone."*

You see, God is a God of strategy too. He changes His strategy all the time and what you did last time in a season of battle might not be what He wants you to do this time around. Use strong discernment and do what the Spirit demands. It is your duty as a good worship leader to help facilitate this for God and your pastor. During the sermon, let your ear be very alert to what the Spirit of the Lord is suggesting as songs that will drive the message that has just been preached home especially if it is upon you to choose the song. If your pastor picks a song, well and good, do it to the best of your ability. This is not the time for you to pick a random song that you heard on radio yesterday to show everyone your vocal agility.

In the same team, I had been entrusted the role of not just leading the team but overseeing worship in the whole church. I am very serious about being in unity with my pastor when it comes to leadership and so as I prepared each week to lead, I always commanded my spirit to be synchronized to the Spirit of the Lord and that of the pastor. I would ask the Holy Spirit to give me songs that were in sync with what the pastor was going to preach each Sunday and sure enough, the Lord did it! It was always amazing how from the beginning of the service the Lord would be confirming the message He had given to the pastor or whoever had been assigned to preach that day using the songs He had given me or whoever I had assigned to lead that day. This will only be accomplished when you as a worship leader know your pastor's spirit. You will be able to pick up what direction they are taking during the service and even in the team. Often times as the preacher of the word came forward and would have a specific song on their heart, because of this prayer to be in sync with each other's spirits and the Spirit of the Lord; it's almost as if I would take the word right off their mouth and lead the song they wanted. This is not a brag sentence but just teaching you how this just makes things easier for you and the pastor. Each win is a win for the entire church.

__*Always go into a service with high expectation of the Lord to move upon your worship*__. A lot of times it is the worship leaders themselves who come to lead without any expectation at all because what they are doing has become such a routine and they are just going through the motions. *"Ugh, just another Sunday… let me run through this thirty minute session and move on to more exciting things.* "By having this kind of attitude, you not only shortchange the Lord, but you the people whom you have been assigned to lead into worship by releasing this lethargic spirit into the atmosphere. And then you want to act surprised when the congregation responds to you in lethargy times two. That's what you released!

Proverbs 23:18 says, *"For surely there is an end; and thine expectation shall not be cut off."* When you as the worship leader come in with high hopes that the Lord is going to move mightily on your worship, it not only puts a demand on the Lord but it gets caught by the people you are leading and they raise their expectation as you are *"leading"* them.

Leading worship is not just when you open your mouth to sing but the attitude and vibe you are also leading with is caught by those that you are leading because you are not only releasing the anointing into the service but your spirit as well.

Expectation is a powerful force. What you expect will come to pass and what you do not expect will never come to pass. There is a super-natural force that draws whatever you are expecting towards you. To *cut off* here, means to be killed. So in literal sense the Bible is saying that no one will kill your expectation because it is yours based on what you have believed. And then the supernatural is added to it now when the Lord comes in. He is committed to your expectation and will make sure it is fulfilled. Learn to tailor them to what God has promised you in His Word.

Worship leaders minister about 80 percent of the services each week. Yes, you do actually minister longer than your pastor. It is there-fore imperative for you to be very continuously prepared. Spend time consistently in the presence of the Lord in private and make sure you have a breakthrough there in worship before you go on to lead. You can never take people where you have not been! Shouting at people and commanding them to worship is not the way to release the spirit of worship. It is what is flowing from you that releases it.

Proverbs 16:1 says, *"The preparations of the heart in man, and the answer of the tongue, is from the Lord."* What this means is that you prepare as led of the Lord and the Holy Spirit determines what comes out of your mouth at that particular moment. Remember when Jesus told the disciples in Luke 12:11-12, *"Do not worry about how or what you should answer, or what you should say, for the Holy Spirit will teach you in that very hour what you ought to say.*" Do your part in preparation and He will breathe upon your songs but do not by any means put any restrictions on Him moving differently during the service. I want you to know that you have your list of songs and Holy Spirit has His list. He is the One who searches the depths of God and He knows what is in the heart and mind of God for that day and His job is to make sure that is fulfilled in our lives and in all services as well. Allow Him to make this happen because all He desires is to see Jesus glorified.

What is your Sunday morning song selection process: If stopped and asked about any of the songs you've chosen for your worship set, could you explain its lyric/content? How has the song ministered to you? I usually find that when a song hasn't ministered to me first it's a little difficult to lead it. When a song ministers to me, it takes my spirit back to a place where the Lord has been what I am singing to Him and how He provided, delivered or even was so awesome to me. So because the message of the song is etched in my spirit, and I remember from whence He has brought me, I find it easier to interpret it into worship out of my inner being.

Spontaneous song is usually introduced by the Holy Spirit during the service and it is important for everyone to be alert so that they know when this has happened. Constantly practicing with your entire team – musicians included, helps everyone learn the different styles of different worship leaders in the team. You know what direction sister A is headed to when she is leading because as you rehearse you also learn each other's spirits. Remember we said earlier that the Spirit of the Lord is not the author of confusion. When He starts a spontaneous song, it will be perfect and easy to catch for the singers, musicians and congregation alike. You can introduce new songs as you go but some of them require more practice.

We used to introduce new songs to the church during offering time and after the benediction prayer. We would do it over and over such that when the new songs were finally introduced to the church; most people in the congregation knew them. There are simple songs that can be taught as the service is going on but all the songs can't be new ones. This is because you are leading- meaning you want people to follow you and sometimes it seems as though worship leaders are up on the altar doing a solo instead of leading. They have five new songs that they seem to be doing their own thing up there with and so the congregation is just watching and then after the service you hear the worship leaders saying how the enemy really resisted them that day. No! You sung songs they did not know. Just change the songs and you will see the difference it makes. There are other times when the congregation just resists new songs and insist that the worship team lead some of their favorite songs. This happens all the time in churches and they would be waiting for you at the door to tell you that that's why they sat down because they didn't like those songs. As a good worship leader, don't make any promises that you cannot keep because you are trying to stay on their favorite list. Remember that we are here to please God and not man.

The Holy Spirt is the greatest worship leader there will ever be and He wants to teach you how to worship! He is the Spirit of Jesus and loves Jesus. He loves to make sure that Jesus is exalted in every worship service and He fills up every room or region where Jesus is being exalted. If this is not the case, the Holy Spirit is absent and you find that you are struggling a whole lot with your leading. The service is also very dry and it is in dry places where the devil likes to dwell.

While leading worship, I usually surrender my ear, emotions and tongue to the Holy Spirit so that He can use me as a conduit to do what He wants to do in that particular moment. Sometimes I don't have a song popping up in my mind even though I had prepared a list but because I probably sensed that He wants to take us in a different direction, I just allow Him to whisper the next song to me. He does it so smoothly and the transition is easier. When it is really Him, there is no confusion. 1 Corinthians 14:33a says, *"for God is not the author of confusion but of peace."*

Always allow room for worship. Most times because of our schedules, we tend to rush on to the next thing on the program and fail to master the art of entertaining the Lord. So, in essence we are saying we want the Lord to manifest Himself amongst us but then when He comes we are very quick to jump on to the next thing on our program. We are like "Oh Lord! That was wonderful but we are sorry we have to go on and preach the word but thanks for coming" We fail to realize that Jesus- the Word Himself is amongst us and once again quench His Spirit. And once again Jesus has to walk out of our buildings that we have built for Him starved of worship. It is no wonder we ourselves are also starved of life itself and are just going through the motions. How can we have a move of God in our lives if we won't even entertain the Lord for a couple of hours? We have the language down of wanting a mighty move of God but when it comes down to the work that goes into it we will not do it. Worship fatigue is rampant in the church today because people don't stretch themselves in the Spirit on their private altars. All we want is entertainment and after a few minutes of worship, a yawn here and another there to signal the worship leaders that they should move on to the next thing. And God forbid they don't lead our favorite songs or allow our favorite singers to sing!

This is why the ***transitions during a worship service have to be handled very gently*** so that we are not quenching the Spirit of the Lord. If the worship session has gone very high and the person handling the next session comes on and cuts off the worship because *we have a lot to do today,* they just quenched the Holy Spirit. Instead, they can encourage the congregation to keep worshiping and allow the Holy Spirit to do what He intends to do with that moment. And because cutting off is usually what happens in most churches, it is imperative that this is taught to every leader, pastors included so that we know how to handle that very sensitive moment.

Another thing we must understand as worship leaders is that ***we are not puppets on a stage or entertainers chosen to entertain anyone.*** We are not in the show business. No matter how many people are in the room, we are there for an *Audience of One.* Jesus our magnificent obsession is *Who* we are here to entertain and please. If you are one of those people who get their fulfilment when the crowd is cheering you on and screaming each time you are on stage because you are entertaining them so well, you will soon find out how fickle human beings are – love you one moment and want to stone you the next. I remember as a teenager soon after I had my son, I went back to church and got back on the worship team but because I had a child out of wedlock and my story was known in the whole village since I was publicly denied and embarrassed, I would get on the altar to lead praise and worship and most times get booed or people would sit down and others would walk out until I was done leading. It was very embarrassing and initially I thought about quitting and just being a regular church member but I remember one Sunday at a crusade the Lord telling me to fix my eyes on Him. So in all the shame and tears, I took the mic and just started praising like crazy just looking at Jesus. I did not care what they said or thought about me. Jesus approved of me and He delighted in my praise and He was there to receive it. I had been accustomed to praising and worshiping Him in private but this time I was doing the same thing only with other people watching. And I do not regret any bit of it because as a young girl, it taught me how to keep my focus on Jesus even through adversity. He would show up to my worship sessions and move the people Himself.

It wasn't long after these public rejection experiences that I noticed that the youth in the village were watching me. I used to go to the church daily to pray at 3 O'clock in the afternoon and it was a thirty minute walk from where we lived. On my way there, they would ask to join me and on the days when they didn't, they would be watching through the windows of the church listening to me pray. There were a lot of drunkards in that particular area but they were also very skilled musicians. Since I was always showing love to them and inviting them into the church to pray with me, they felt safe around me and most of them got saved and started following me again to church and asked me if they could join the worship team. I wasn't in charge of it so I presented them to the church leaders and every instrument you can name, they came in and started playing it in the church and now the youth in the area wanted to be part of this group so much. We went around the village in every home evangelizing and many souls came to Christ.

A lot of the same people who had rejected me so badly and even told their sons and daughters that they should never be seen with me now started coming to me to thank me for being instrumental in their children's lives and those whose children still had not changed asked me to help them. I still keep in touch with most of them who call me mum to this day and I thank the Lord for this rigorous training and for choosing me to part of a mighty move of God in my village.

Develop substance to yourself on and off of the altar. Also understand that someone is watching and learning from you whether you like it or not. There are those mentees we choose for ourselves and there are those who glean from us from a distance. The latter are watching you without your knowledge. They follow your every move and posts on social media. They follow your advice and recommendations. They learn from your life. It could be a child or someone who watches your church live stream each Sunday. What message are you sharing with them? You have been given an amazing opportunity to affect and influence lives on a weekly basis. The question here is what are you teaching? Take your assignment seriously and be faithful to it. Give yourself wholly to it.

Luke 16:10-12,

10 "One who is faithful in a very little is also faithful in much, and one who is dishonest in a very little is also dishonest in much. 11 If then you have not been faithful in the unrighteous wealth, who will entrust to you the true riches? 12 And if you have not been faithful in that which is another's, who will give you that which is your own?"

Be faithful and consistent to the Lord and your pastor as well. Take your assignment seriously! You can be so anointed and gifted – I mean oil dripping all over you and another person not as gifted as you are, but faithful to the assignment. They give themselves wholeheartedly to the assignment. In this case, the faithful person is more powerful than the anointed person because as they stay with it consistently trusting the Lord, He is not unjust, they will get better with time. A faithful person can get anointed but an unfaithful anointed person is a dangerous person to have on your team. Most of the latter will use anything as an excuse to be inconsistent and will then get very offended when they are corrected. If the worship team leader does not catch this behavior early and cut if off at the root, they will be raising a big, big monster that they might not be able to kill later. Some of them are just too gifted they have never had anyone correct them because they are afraid they will leave the team so they are used to getting away with certain behavior. This spirit is rampant in the church but we are talking about worship teams here. This is why every team leader needs to know those they are leading so that in such a case you can cut off certain behavior early and lead them in the right direction. Some of them though, as you will learn along the way, you just have to release from the team.

David didn't start out as a skillful player, but he stayed with it. Daily perfecting his skill until he became a master at it. I have noticed that there is a lot of indiscipline on people who feel that they are gifted and don't need to work as hard as everyone else, eventually these end up losing even what they had in the first place.

Another thing, please ***be yourself!*** When you are entrusted to lead people in worship, this is not the time to prove that you are the Aretha Franklin of your time. There will only be one Aretha Franklin and she is resting in peace right now. Stop these antics of trying to prove yourself to people. Especially in the age of social media, you want to do a four minute clip singing like Aretha and you have asked someone in the congregation to take a video of it and post it for you. Stop it! Be yourself. Trying to mimic someone else is an injustice to God and yourself. ***You have your own sound that the Lord wants you to release into the earth*** and as long as you're working overtime to prove that you are Aretha Franklin, you will never find it. ***Stay faithful to your sound.*** If only we worked as hard to be like Jesus as we do celebrities!

Invest in your team by giving them opportunities to work their gifts. Don't be an insecure leader who holds back the gifts that God has sent them. All those gifts have been sent to edify the church. Be so confident in the Lord that whoever He tells you to give a chance you go ahead and do it. Also, pray for your team members individually. There are times when you will pick up something about your team members in the Spirit when you constantly pray for them. There is this strategy I taught in my team called the ***surround method.*** I taught how to do this each time we sensed that something was going on with anyone of us. So we would surround the individual and pray in the Spirit until whatever was weighing them down was lifted. I think it is a great method to implement in your team so that each person can learn how to be sensitive to the other. As for conflict management, try as much as possible not to handle this before going on the altar because it contaminates the heart and flow of worship. If it is something that can be talked about after the service, take care of it then because I've found that when this is done prior to going on the altar, it diverts everyone's attention to the issue instead of worship. Some things are too serious and cannot be taken to the altar so it is upon you to judge wisely as a leader. Others however, can be taken care of after ministering.

Lastly, as a worship team leader, understand that you are a watchman and what you allow to come into the team will come in. Keep your spirit alert for who and what is coming in.

CHAPTER 7

Guarding your heart

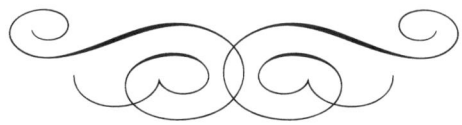

As a worshiper, one of the most important things to you is purity of the heart because it is from the activity that is going on in your heart that can dictate and pour out into a lot of things in your life. Purity of heart and body is very necessary for one to be a true worshipper. You can't harbor stuff in your heart and expect a breakthrough.

On this chapter, I want us to focus on guarding your heart as a worshiper. What we do as worshipers comes from our hearts and so, if your heart is not right, then your worship is not right. Whatever you allow in your heart will determine what comes out of your mouth and life in general. The Bible says in Luke 6:45 "*A good man out of the good treasure of his heart bringeth forth that which is good; and an evil man out of the evil treasure of his heart bringeth forth that which is evil: for of the abundance of the heart his mouth speaketh.*"

You have to protect you heart so that it doesn't become bitter, contaminated and eventually defile your worship. One time Jesus was accused by the Pharisees that His disciples did not wash their hands before they ate. They believed that over the course of the day the hands get defiled by many things and so before one could eat; they had to wash their hands. In response to that question, Jesus gave an answer that helps us identify where the issue is. Matthew 15:11 says, *"Not what goes into the mouth defiles a man; but what comes out of the mouth, this defiles a man."* 17-20 says, *"Do you not yet understand that whatever enters the mouth goes into the stomach and is eliminated? But those things which proceed out of the mouth come from the heart, and they defile a man. For out of the heart proceed evil thoughts, murders, adulteries, fornications, thefts, false witness, and blasphemies.*

These are the things which defile a man, but to eat with unwashed hands does not defile a man." So, according to Jesus' answer, we see that defilement does not come from what you eat physically but by what comes out of your heart. Spiritual defilement comes from our hearts, expressed through our words and manifested in our lives. Now we see why the quality of your heart is very important to the totality of worship as a lifestyle because it will soon overflow in every area of your life. If you don't keep your heart right, you cannot worship right.

In Proverbs NIV 4:23, the Bible says, *"Above all else, guard your heart, for everything you do flows from it"* other versions say, *"Guard your heart with all diligence for out of it spring the issues of life."* The heart in this scripture is compared to a spring or a river. Again we see that the things that really impact our lives flow from within not without. The condition of your heart determines the quality of your worship and life in general. Just like the physical heart is responsible for circulating blood throughout your body. So if you do not guard your heart, you will contaminate your worship. The instruction here is to make every effort to keep our hearts pure. We must be intentional about this! So as a worship leader, if your heart is not right and you're leading people into worship, the life or death that is in you is what you are releasing into the atmosphere. Everything about you on the outside might look perfect but it's really the activity of the heart that determines what is released.

This is the part of man that we don't see with our natural eye that controls the man – the heart. It is distinguished from our appearance. No wonder the Lord told Samuel when he had gone to anoint the sons of Jesse in 1 Samuel 16:7

"But the Lord said to Samuel, "Do not look at his appearance or at his physical stature, because I have refused him. For the Lord does not see as man sees; for man looks at the outward appearance, but the Lord looks at the heart."

One of the components of the heart is devotion - The part of man that leads him to worship or express allegiance to someone or something. This is where we give our lives in total submission to something. It comes from deep within the heart. This could be a sport, belief, politics or someone. Their sense of worship is directed to that one thing and they give their all to it. This is why we have to be careful who we give our hearts to. Be diligent and deliberate in keeping your heart. You will notice many times in the Bible that the heart and the spirit are used interchangeably and, in this context, they mean the same thing. For example, Ezekiel 11:19 says, *"Then I will give them one heart, and I will put a new spirit within them, and take the stony heart out of their flesh, and give them a heart of flesh* and also in Romans 2:29, the Bible says, "*but he is a Jew who is one inwardly; and circumcision is that of the heart, in the Spirit, not in the letter; whose praise is not from men but from God.*"

So, if we have to keep our hearts with all diligence, what are some of the ways that things can enter or leave our hearts? Guarding here implies that there is a door or gate to the heart and as we all know, doors are two-way, for entrance or exit. There are three ways that things enter into your heart. First is through words, images, and experiences. At every turn, someone is trying to win your heart whether you know it or not.

It could be through a commercial, song or words so it is up to you to be extremely vigilant. This is why for example, commercials are not just run one time but for a period of time targeting the same people and making sure they see or hear it again and again in an effort to make you be devoted to it. You are where you are today because of what you allowed to enter into your heart.

Now, let's deal with something that is rampant in worshipers and the Body of Christ as a whole. This is offense and the process of how it enters the heart, and defiles a man or woman. Remember that we are trying to identify the things that can clog our worship and going to the root of it at the heart level so that we can maintain a pure posture of worship before the Lord. I couldn't think about a better example than that of Judas Iscariot about a week before the Passover. It is also very interesting to me that this incident is from one of my favorite displays of extravagant worship in the Bible. I have expounded this on the chapter on extravagant worship. John 12:4-8 says, *"But one of His disciples, Judas Iscariot, Simon's son, who would betray Him, said, "Why was this fragrant oil not sold for three hundred denarii and given to the poor?" This he said, not that he cared for the poor, but because he was a thief, and had the money box; and he used to take what was put in it. But Jesus said, "Let her alone; [she has kept this for the day of My burial. For the poor you have with you always, but Me you do not have always."*

Jesus was in the house of Lazarus and a woman came and poured precious ointment on the feet of Jesus as she wiped it with her hair. This extravagant display of worship resulted in some misgivings from some of the disciples including Judas. In this process, we are going to look at four things that led him to do what he did. The first one was that he was rebuked by Jesus – openly.

The words *"leave her alone"* literally mean *"Shut up!"* Jesus publicly rebuked Judas after his suggestion. What happens when someone rebukes you publicly? Well, Judas didn't take it lightly. Remember this was six days before Passover. The day before, he hadn't planned to betray Jesus but this day after the rebuke, he made up his mind to betray him (Although we know that this had already been in motion since the foundation of the earth so that Jesus would die for our sins) We know however, that he wasn't the only person that was rebuked by Jesus. Actually, the person that got more rebukes was Peter with Jesus even saying *"get thee behind me Satan"* at one time, but for some reason, Peter never took offense and he never stopped loving the Lord. He would move on and learn his lesson. Just think about how you would have acted had you been in the hot seat as many times as Peter was. Would you have served in Jesus' ministry or would you have dropped out because of offense? Peter had such a good character about this such that even when the Lord had given them the chance to drop out he would not! But Simon Peter answered Him, *"Lord, to whom shall we go? You have the words of eternal life. Also we have come to believe and know that You are the Christ, the Son of the living God."* John 6:60-71 *"Therefore many of His disciples, when they heard this, said, "This is a hard saying; who can understand it?" When Jesus knew in Himself that His disciples [complained about this, He said to them, "Does this offend you? What then if you should see the Son of Man ascend where He was before? It is the Spirit who gives life; the flesh profits nothing. The words that I speak to you are spirit, and they are life. But there are some of you who do not believe." For Jesus knew from the beginning who they were who did not believe, and who would betray Him. And He said, "Therefore I have said to you that no one can come to Me unless it has been granted to him by My Father." From that time many of His disciples went back and walked with Him no more. Then Jesus said to the twelve, "Do you also want to go away?" But Simon Peter answered Him, "Lord, to whom shall we go? You have the words of eternal life. Also we have come to believe and know that You are the Christ, the Son of the living God." Jesus answered them, "Did I not choose you, the twelve, and one of you is a devil?" He spoke of Judas Iscariot; the son of Simon, for it was he who would betray Him, being one of the twelve."*

It is also important to note that it is here when Jesus mentions offense that he brought up who would later betray Him.

There are some people who can't stand being corrected or rebuked! They always want praise and affirmation and if they don't get it, they fly off the hinges. So now, Judas has been rebuked and he takes it personally and the next thing we see is that he gets a satanic idea and he entertains it because he's bitter from the rebuke he got a while ago. At this moment, his heart has been defiled by offense and bitterness. He made a decision that he would betray Jesus. When people get to this point, they can't be stopped. The Bible says that immediately after the bread he went out *and it was night* in short trying to say that his heart had turned dark or darkness had descended upon his heart. He did not guard his heart! I believe that we are now seeing the importance of keeping our hearts pure so that we can worship the Lord in Spirit and in Truth. What have you allowed in your heart? One of the greatest tactics that the enemy uses in the Body of Christ to defile worshipers and believers a whole is offense and bitterness. You have to make up your mind to forgive quickly like Peter and move on! A forgiving heart is esteemed higher than a gift offered from a heart of bitterness.

The Bible says in Hebrews 12:15b, "*lest any root of bitterness springing up cause trouble, and by this many become defiled*" A lot of people are walking around defiled and not even knowing it! Bitterness will clog up the river of living water that is supposed to flow and bring life to you and others when you worship. And you find that instead of releasing life, death is coming out. This is especially important for worshipers who have a platform to lead others into worship. Bitterness starts out as an offense at first and then it keeps eating at someone's heart finally blocking the flow of one's river. You cannot worship like this!

There are two types of people- Those who have rule over their spirit or heart, and those who don't. The first group is found in Proverbs 25:28 where the Bible says, "*Whoever has no rule over his own spirit is like a city broken down, without walls.*" Meaning that they are passive and they leave their hearts and spirits unguarded. The second group is found in Proverbs 16:32, "*He who is slow to anger is better than the mighty, and he who rules his spirit than he who takes a city.*" They have learned to move beyond emotion, hurt and pain.

Which one of these are you? Take a moment and examine your heart today and take charge in the name of Jesus to guard your heart so that only life will flow from it.

CHAPTER 8

Redirecting Your Passion

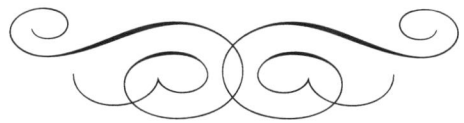

If you are a worshiper, you will notice that you have passion, and lots of it, and if it is not channeled in the right direction, it is the very thing that the enemy will try to use against you. He tried multiple times to contaminate my worship from an early age so that I could run after vanities. Yes, I have struggled terribly, but I was also very willing to allow His strength to be made perfect in my weakness. One of the things I learnt about the Lord is that even though He knows about our weaknesses and the things that we are so ashamed of, it is such a surrendering thing to go to Him nakedly and admit that "Yes Lord, I am weak in this area, but if You can cleanse me and use me, I am all Yours! "I found that it is very important to always have a "yes" in your spirit towards the Lord. The Lord is not after the perfect, but the willing. If you tell Him *"Yes Lord I know I struggle in these areas, but I am still available to You"*. He will use you and help you through whatever it is that you're going through. He already knows your struggle, but it is so much more powerful when you openly talk to Him about it. 2 Corinthians 12:8-9 says, *"Concerning this thing I pleaded with the Lord three times that it might depart from me. And He said to me, "My grace is sufficient for you, for My strength is made perfect in weakness." Therefore most gladly I will rather boast in my infirmities, that the power of Christ may rest upon me."*

As time goes by, those things that have consumed us so much end up getting consumed in our pursuit of the Lover of our souls. This is where true freedom begins.

I fought through all my weaknesses for my relationship with the Lord to stand. I had a willing heart to work with the Lord. I watched over and over as His strength became perfect in my weaknesses. My passion caused me to run after Him and nothing could stop me. Sure there have been lots of times when I failed in this but I stood up, dusted myself and got back on track. I watched myself progress from the outer court into the Holy of holies where I lay prostrate at the feet of my Master in total adoration.

Again, in writing this, I do not try to portray myself as an angel, but as a human being with many, many flaws, yet whom the Lord has chosen to minister to Him this day. Being intimately acquainted with my own deficiencies has kept me in a posture of worship because I am ever aware of my constant need for Him. As Paul writes in 2 Corinthians 4:7-12 MSG, *"If you only look at us, you might well miss the brightness. We carry this precious Message around in the unadorned clay pots of our ordinary lives. That's to prevent anyone from confusing God's incomparable power with us. As it is, there's not much chance of that. You know for yourselves that we're not much to look at. We've been surrounded and battered by troubles, but we're not demoralized; we're not sure what to do, but we know that God knows what to do; we've been spiritually terrorized, but God hasn't left our side; we've been thrown down, but we haven't broken. What they did to Jesus, they do to us—trial and torture, mockery and murder; what Jesus did among them, he does in us—he lives! Our lives are at constant risk for Jesus' sake, which makes Jesus' life all the more evident in us. While we're going through the worst, you're getting in on the best!"*

Yes, I might have thought that others were better for what had been given to me, but 1 Corinthians 1:27 states that "**He uses the foolish things of this world to put to shame the wise.**" For me to fulfill all His will, I had to be dependent on Him fully. Every time I took my eyes off of Him and thought I was strong enough to make it on my own, something would knock me off my high horse and remind me again that I am nothing without Him.

On most days as I write this book, I have stopped to weep and just marvel at His goodness as I allow the things He has taught me through painful seasons be released to you this day. Do not ever discount yourself or allow anyone else to. The outcasts of today are usually the appointed and anointed ones for tomorrow!

2 Corinthians 1:4 says, "God of all healing counsel! He comes alongside us when we go through hard times, and before you know it, he brings us alongside someone else who is going through hard times so that we can be there for that person just as God was there for us." Receive them from Him as you allow Him to minister to your spirit and just cry out to Him in your weakness and tell Him *Lord, I am available for You to use me as You will. I give You my past, present and future, use it for Your glory!*

The journey into the depths of worship is not a cheap one, it will cost you *everything* to worship as it is through the furnaces of affliction that the worshiper learns to fix his or her eyes on the Lord rather than on the fire. As life beats you up over and over again, you will have only one story to tell…His faithfulness! You can't learn this stuff in a class. You have to go through some stuff where the pure gold will be separated from the dross and until He sees His image in you, He will keep putting you back on the potter's vessel.

2 Timothy 2:20-21 says, "But *in a great house there are not only vessels of gold and silver, but also of wood and clay, some for honor and some for dishonor. Therefore, if anyone cleanses himself from the latter, he will be a vessel for honor, sanctified and useful for the Master, prepared for every good work.*" It is during this process of submitting yourself to the process of the Lord for you that He makes you into a vessel of honor and teaches you to worship Him.

I remember one time I was going through such a tough season and though I have learned to seek the Lord and learn through what I am going through, I complained so much to the Lord that particular Sunday morning and told Him how tired I was of whatever I was going through. I went as far as to point out that I didn't want to be part of it and demanded that I get pulled out immediately. I was the one leading worship that morning and when I stepped on the altar I was so over-whelmed by the presence of the Lord and the Holy Spirit as He wept started saying in my ear, *"He is faithful!" "He is Faithful!"* and so I started saying it out loud as I led worship and it got to the point where the Holy Spirit gave me a stern warning that no matter what I found myself in or how bad I thought it was, that Jesus is **always faithful** and I should never say anything else but to judge Him faithful. It was such an intense moment that took over the entire worship session. Moments later, the preacher stood up and her message was **He is faithful**. I rejoiced in the Lord and repented for letting discouragement sneak into my heart that morning. He was letting me know even in that moment that He is faithful.

May the Holy Spirit reach out to you right now as you read this and reveal to you the purpose of what you are going through. May He lead you from the outer court into the Holy of holies where His manifest presence dwells. Forget about yourself for a moment and focus your eyes on Him and say unto Him that "even in this situation Lord, I judge You faithful!"

Do not discount yourself because you think that you're not good enough or you think that someone else is fit for the job. Throughout the Bible we find that God's choosing criteria is very different from ours. What is famous with Him is not so popular with us and what is famous with us does not make it to His books. Just learn to avail yourself to Him and watch Him use the very thing that was bringing you down as a stepping stone in your life! I am not one of those mighty singers who have crazy vocal ability and sure enough, someone else would have been fit for the job especially in the age that we are living in full of amazing talent. But the Lord was not interested in all that I had to show but the activity of my heart. I love to worship Him! I have no one else but Him.

In the story of David the shepherd, this principle is highly emphasized. 1 Samuel 13:14 *"But now your kingdom shall not continue. The Lord has sought for Himself a man after His own heart, and the Lord has commanded him to be commander over His people, because you have not kept what the Lord commanded you."*

In this passage when the Lord talks about finding Himself a man after His own heart, He did not mean perfect man but a man after the pattern of His heart. This brings us back to the scripture about God seeking out true worshipers who worship Him in Spirit and in Truth. It is implied here that the Lord had gone on a hunt and His eyes were roaming to and fro upon the earth seeking for someone after His heart. His eyes were over the wilderness of Bethlehem at this particular moment when His ears heard some music playing and His eyes saw a young boy by the name of David playing his harp and singing about the goodness of the Lord and how he longed to be in His presence all the days of His life. There was no one there with him but a herd off sheep. I can see the Lord stopping everything and drawing closer to David in a lot of excitement. He shut out all the other music from nature and the birds and was just soaking up the worship from David. Then the Lord exclaimed, *"I have found Myself a man after Mine own heart! He is singing Me, telling Me I am his Waymaker, his shield and his everything. I will make him king over My children Israel!"*

This is so amazing to me. When Saul was so busy seeing position, David was in the wilderness of Judah seeking the presence of the Lord as he kept his father's sheep. In complete obscurity! I mean, who goes looking for someone in the desert? It is an uninhabited and silent place from a human standpoint. Yet David was never alone. The Lord was always with Him, enjoying his worship and also speaking to Him. Let me tell you dear reader, this is the power of worship. It will have you pulled out of the trenches and set on the throne. This is the case in my life too. I come from an extremely poor and small village in Kenya Africa. According to man, I shouldn't be here. Yet here I am writing to you today. People from where I am from never made it too far but by His grace here, I am today! All I knew to do was worship. I must have looked like a fool to many praising and worshiping the Lord with a handheld drum in the hot sun and getting lost in His presence, but it was not in vain! Look what the Lord has done! Obscurity does not limit God. As a matter of fact, it sets up a stage for Him to demonstrate His power when He raises us up to honor and prominence. I completely relate to David's story and I can attest that power belongs to God! The Lord is not promoting position seekers but presence seekers so He rejected Saul. He found Himself a man after His own heart. Not perfect, not clean according to the standards of man, not after the pattern of His heart but after His heart.1 Sam 2:30b says, *"for those who honor Me I will honor, and those who despise Me shall be lightly esteemed."*

It is not hard for us to notice the type of rejection David went through with his family. It is even expressed in the way that his older brothers talk to him and how his own father had brought out all the sons for Samuel's anointing ceremony but had somehow *"forgotten"* David. For the family to be in such a moment of honor, one would think that Jesse would have wanted all of his children to have the privilege of being part of this important event. Yet this was not the case. Can you imagine what that must have done to little David? Not to even get acceptance from his own father? Although by now- at sixteen years old,

I don't think it was such a big surprise for him to be rejected by his own family. He had gotten used to it. It probably wasn't the first party at the family house that he didn't get invited to. Samuel, a seasoned prophet had made the same mistake we all make by looking at the stature of the sons of Jesse and chosen from the outside appearance or credentials. 1 Samuel 16 *When they arrived, Samuel saw Eliab and thought, "Surely the Lord's anointed stands here before the Lord. "But the Lord said to Samuel, "Do not consider his appearance or his height, for I have rejected him. The Lord does not look at the things people look at. People look at the outward appearance, but the Lord looks at the heart. "Then Jesse called Abinadab and had him pass in front of Samuel. But Samuel said, "The Lord has not chosen this one either. "Jesse then had Shammah pass by, but Samuel said, "Nor has the Lord chosen this one. "Jesse had seven of his sons pass before Samuel, but Samuel said to him, "The Lord has not chosen these. "So he asked Jesse, "Are these all the sons you have?" There is still the youngest," Jesse answered. "He is tending the sheep." Samuel said, "Send for him; we will not sit down until he arrives. "So he sent for him and had him brought in. He was glowing with health and had a fine appearance and handsome features. Then the Lord said, "Rise and anoint him; this is the one." So Samuel took the horn of oil and anointed him in the presence of his brothers, and from that day on the Spirit of the Lord came powerfully upon David. Samuel then went to Ramah."*

If you make yourself available to the Lord in private, no matter what is going on in your life, the Lord will make sure that wherever you are supposed to be in your destiny, that you get there. He also honors you and shows you off in public as you do to Him in private. Those who rejected you will have to stand up till you arrive like they did for young

David. The Lord Himself will see to it. Just be available to Him. This goes to explain the psalm 23:5 which says, *"Thou prepares a table for me in the presence of mine enemies; Thou anointest my head with oil."*

Another thing I'd like to talk about is relationships. Since worshipers are relational beings and are always seeking the Lord, the enemy knows this and he is always trying to introduce counterfeit relationships to you to keep you distracted from the main thing which is seeking the Lord. He plants someone in your life who will keep you busy enough so that you no longer have time to spend with the Lord. In some cases he even succeeds in taking your purity of body from you by setting you up in sexual relationships. All this is to pacify you so that you will not realize what you really need is the Lord. If you find yourself in such a situation, I would advise you to talk to someone you trust about it who and help you get back on track. Be careful who you talk to because some people in the church are in the tell-all business not for the profit of the Body but for their own gain and preying on the weaknesses of others. Also understand that with you being a worshiper, the devil hates you because you are doing what he can no longer do and will do everything in his power to bring you down. His intention is to set you up in stuff so that he can disgrace you the same way he was disgraced. He fights worshipers very hard but it is all because of jealousy because they are doing what he used to do before he was thrown out of heaven. Having this in mind, let us strive to live a pure life before the Lord and not leave any open door that he can use in our lives. Also constantly examine your heart and repent before the Lord and make up in your mind that you will redirect your passion to Him again.

CHAPTER 9

Shifting atmospheres

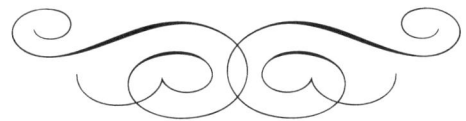

I learned a very important lesson on shifting atmospheres during my leadership tenure at a certain church. It is how your worship can affect not only your household but shift entire atmospheres and regions causing breakthroughs to you and the people in it.

It began simply by some Sundays being easier while on others it felt as if the enemy had exerted himself all over the place making it impossible for us to have a breakthrough. In these moments the Lord taught me how to use praise to break the resistance of the enemy. You see when you're praising, you are exalting and magnifying the Lord and like I said earlier, magnifying the Lord does not make Him any bigger than He already is but it makes Him bigger than your situation and in this case, the resistance you are facing.

I noticed that in these times most of us spend more time binding and rebuking the enemy instead of focusing on Jesus. One day the Lord told me, *"Tell your team not to spend so much time fighting with the enemy. He likes the attention. Teach them how to magnify Me in resistance and I will fill up the room."* So, we changed our strategy. I am not diminishing the importance of putting the enemy in his place but as we do this, let us not put too much attention on him and end up losing the focus of why we are gathered in the first place. If we make sure the Lord is lifted high amongst us, everything else will have to bow down and the only way to enthrone the Lord amongst us is through praise. Psalm 149:5-9,

> *"Let the saints be joyful in glory;*
> *Let them sing aloud on their beds.*
> *Let the high praises of God be in their mouth,*
> *And a two-edged sword in their hand,*
> *To execute vengeance on the nations,*
> *And punishments on the peoples;*
> *To bind their kings with chains,*
> *And their nobles with fetters of iron;*
> *To execute on them the written judgment—*
> *This honor have all His saints. Praise the Lord!"*

In the above text, we find that when the high praises of God are in our mouths, it is as if we have two edged sword in our hand and are executing vengeance on the nations, binding their kings with chains and their nobles with fetters of iron. What an honor! The two edged sword here also represents the word of God. So, when you come into a resistant atmosphere, lift up the high praise of God and you will be arresting every evil force and inviting the Lord into the building. Remember that Lord is enthroned in the praises of His people.

> *Psalm 22:3,*
> *"But You are holy,*
> *Enthroned in the praises of Israel."*

As I spoke earlier about how the Lord broke into the cell that Paul and Silas were in not because they were singing so well but because He is enthroned in the praises of His people, when you start praising Him no matter what condition you're in, He will break into that situation. The doors of the cell opening were just an announcement that He had come into the room and He cannot be jailed!

> In Psalm 108:8,
> *"Gilead is mine, Manasseh is mine;*
> *Ephraim is my helmet,*
> *Judah is my scepter."*

According to Merriam Webster, *a scepter is a staff or baton borne by a sovereign as an emblem of authority.* What this means is that Judah is a representative of God's authority and power. So, in essence when you praise, you are bringing the authority and power into your life and the region that you are in.

Let's look at another passage on the power of praise. Gen 49:8-12 says,

> *"Judah, your brothers will praise you;*
> *your hand will be on the neck of your enemies;*
> *your father's sons will bow down to you.*

You are a lion's cub, Judah;
you return from the prey, my son.
Like a lion he crouches and lies down,
like a lioness—who dares to rouse him?
The scepter will not depart from Judah,
nor the ruler's staff from between his feet,
until he to whom it belongs shall come
and the obedience of the nations shall be his.
He will tether his donkey to a vine,
his colt to the choicest branch;
he will wash his garments in wine,
his robes in the blood of grapes.
His eyes will be darker than wine,
his teeth whiter than milk."

Again, we see that through praise our hand will be on the neck of our enemies and that the scepter shall not depart from Judah (Praise). So now when you get into that environment that seems hard, stop talking or worrying and just praise and watch the authority of God come into it. When God comes in, the devil must leave!

Praise confuses the enemy because he just can't understand why you are praising during difficulty. He wants you to stand up there and fuss at everyone for "*not praising God*" which, if truth be told, you are not doing either because you are now transferring your anxiety on everyone. Ignore the enemy and praise! We see this very clearly in 2 Chronicles 20:21-25,

"When he had consulted with the people, he appointed those who sang to the Lord and those who praise Him in their holy (priestly) attire, as they went out before the army and said, "Praise and give thanks to the Lord, for His mercy and lovingkindness endure forever." When they began singing and praising, the Lord set ambushes against the sons of Ammon, Moab, and Mount Seir, who had come against Judah; so they were struck down (in defeat). For the sons of Ammon and Moab rose up against the inhabitants of Mount Seir, completely destroying them; and when they had finished with the inhabitants of Seir, they helped destroy one another. When the men of Judah came to the lookout tower of the wilderness, they looked towards the multitude, and behold, they were dead bodies lying on the ground and no one had escaped. When Jehoshaphat and his people came to take their spoil, they found much among them, including equipment, garments, and valuable things which they took for themselves, more than they could carry away; so much that they spent three days gathering the spoil."

The first thing I noticed when I started reading this passage is the Ammonites and Moabites *decided to make war against Jehoshaphat who was the leader of the tribe of Judah.* How can you invade someone or rather a tribe who the Lord says hold His scepter as we saw earlier in this chapter? Clearly, these guys did not do their homework on who they were about to attack! If they had, they would have learned all the dangerous prophetic promises God had bestowed on Judah and stayed in the countries. No wonder they got so confused and whooped each other left and right and all Judah had to do was come and collect the spoil and did not have to lift up a finger because the moment they started singing and praising the Lord, He came down and set up ambushes against their enemies. This should make you very confident when you are praising that whatever is opposing you will be ambushed by the Lord Himself and all you have to do is collect the spoils.

As a worship leader, don't spend too much time badgering the congregation to praise or worship. Keep the main thing, the main thing. If you don't take your eyes off of this the enemy will be playing games with you by frustrating your every effort. You don't have to take people on a guilt trip for them to worship the Lord. There is no amount of this that will ever help an unprepared person to worship the Lord because as we have seen in previous chapters, it has to be a lifestyle and a choice that one has to make for themselves. It is a personal thing that has to be going on in the heart of an individual and Sunday service is just an overflow of that. Yes, as a worship leader you can make a suggestion that may lead people into worship and praise but you cannot do it for them. Refrain from taking people on guilt trips so that they can engage in worship. If someone is not grateful for the legs they have, you don't have to tell them that their legs might get cut off if they do not dance for the Lord. I know this sounds funny but we have seen it all.

Don't feel bad that people are not worshiping if you have done your part. Oft times people will blame the worship team *"Oh, you guys didn't sing my favorite song today… why didn't sister A lead today?"* remember we are here to please only One! You will be rigorously tested in this area. The Lord will want to see where your focus is – Him or the people. What makes your heart hurt? When the people don't worship or when you don't please Him? Who are you bringing attention to – Him or yourself?

The Lord God is very jealous and His glory He will not share with another.

Isaiah 42:8 *"I am the Lord, that is My name;*
And My glory I will not give to another,
Nor My praise to carved images."

We are to point all the attention to Jesus! He is the Celebrity. Let's make it clear here. If when you're leading worship most the attention is on you, then you are just worshiping yourself and leading others into it as well. You need to stop this before something terrible happens to you. We have this culture nowadays where we have made gods for ourselves and named them worship leaders just because they are famous and we want some type of influence with them. It is not wrong to celebrate people but when we put them so high that we don't know who we are praising, it is a sin. So, when you as worship leader notice that people are doing this to you, lay all that praise down and give it to Jesus. Remind them that it is Jesus and not you by pointing them back to Him. It is not unusual for people to want to thank you for leading them into powerful praise or worship; it encourages you as a person to keep doing what you are doing but just remember to give Him all that credit. Failing to give God the glory can end up very dangerously as we see in Acts 12:22. *"So on a set day Herod, arrayed in royal apparel, sat on his throne and gave an oration to them. 22 And the people kept shouting, "The voice of a god and not of a man!" 23 Then immediately an angel of the Lord struck him, because he did not give glory to God. And he was eaten by worms and died."*

The consistency of your lifestyle before the Lord is what will command your surroundings. Living a pure life before the Lord and also prayer and worship before the Lord on a daily basis separates you from the person who does it just when they feel like it, or those who do it when they are in trouble. When you stay faithful in the presence of the Lord in private and public, atmospheres must bow down. They will bow down because they recognize the Kingdom you are carrying within you – or in other words the presence of God.

Demons recognize carriers of the glory. See 1 Samuel 5:1-5,

"Then the Philistines took the ark of God and brought it from Ebenezer to Ashdod. When the Philistines took the ark of God, they brought it into the house of Dagon and set it by Dagon. And when the people of Ashdod arose early in the morning, there was Dagon, fallen on its face to the earth before the ark of the Lord. So they took Dagon and set it in its place again. 4 And when they arose early the next morning, there was Dagon, fallen on its face to the ground before the ark of the Lord. The head of Dagon and both the palms of its hands were broken off on the threshold; only Dagon's torso was left of it. Therefore neither the priests of Dagon nor any who come into Dagon's house tread on the threshold of Dagon in Ashdod to this day."

Do not be like the children of Israel who only wanted to use the ark of the Lord during the battle but ignored Him the rest of the days and lived as they pleased. They didn't get defeated because the ark of the Lord was not powerful but because this was not their lifestyle so I believe the Lord was making that statement to them that *"you will not use Me for your convenience!"*

1 Samuel 4:1-11 says, *"Now Israel went out to battle against the Philistines and encamped beside Ebenezer; and the Philistines encamped in Aphek. 2 Then the Philistines put themselves in battle array against Israel. And when they joined battle, Israel was defeated by the Philistines, who killed about four thousand men of the army in the field. And when the people had come into the camp, the elders of Israel said, "Why has the Lord defeated us today before the Philistines? Let us bring the ark of the covenant of the Lord from Shiloh to us, that when it comes among us it may save us from the hand of our enemies." So the people sent to Shiloh, that they might bring from there the ark of the covenant of the Lord of hosts, who dwells between the cherubim. And the two sons of Eli, Hophni and Phinehas, were there with the ark of the covenant of God.*

And when the ark of the covenant of the Lord came into the camp, all Israel shouted so loudly that the earth shook. Now when the Philistines heard the noise of the shout, they said, "What does the sound of this great shout in the camp of the Hebrews mean?" Then they understood that the ark of the Lord had come into the camp. So the Philistines were afraid, for they said, "God has come into the camp!" And they said, "Woe to us! For such a thing has never happened before. Woe to us! Who will deliver us from the hand of these mighty gods? These are the gods who struck the Egyptians with all the plagues in the wilderness. Be strong and conduct yourselves like men, you Philistines that you do not become servants of the Hebrews, as they have been to you. Conduct yourselves like men, and fight!"

So the Philistines fought, and Israel was defeated, and every man fled to his tent. There was a very great slaughter, and there fell of Israel thirty thousand foot soldiers. Also the ark of God was captured; and the two sons of Eli, Hophni and Phinehas, died."

Some worship leaders and even preachers are like this. They ignore the Lord until when they are asked to lead and then that's when they now want to seek Him with intensity so that *He can show up and show out on Sunday morning* and guess for whose glory? Their own! God will not be mocked! 1 Samuel 2:30b says, "but *now the Lord says: 'Far be it from Me; for those who honor Me I will honor, and those who despise Me shall be lightly esteemed."* I hope this helps you make up in your mind that you will consistently seek the Lord in your private lifestyle and watch Him walk up with you on the stages on man.

> Jeremiah 2:27b-28a ,
> *"For they have turned their back to Me, and not their face.*
> *But in the time of their trouble*
> *They will say, 'Arise and save us.'*
> *But where are your gods that you have made for yourselves?*
> *Let them arise, If they can save you in the time of your trouble;"*

Musicians

Another way that shifts the atmosphere is when the musicians play to the Lord way before the service starts. There is power when the musicians come in one accord and just play before the Lord. The Lord loves this and He comes to listen and this creates a brooding of the Holy Spirit in the room. This also prepares the ground before the service starts and makes it easier for the worship leaders since you now come in and continue with the flow already created in the Spirit. Also, when musicians are playing in the Spirit, demons are evil spirits are driven out as seen in 1 Samuel 16:15-16. "*And Saul's servants said to him, "Surely, a distressing spirit from God is troubling you. Let our master now command your servants, who are before you, to seek out a man who is a skillful player on the harp. And it shall be that he will play it with his hand when the distressing spirit from God is upon you, and you shall be well."*

Minstrels command sound and atmospheres and they also set the mood in the rooms. We can see this in the example of David setting the atmosphere when Saul was being tormented by an evil spirit. It is very important that minstrels also develop the art of playing prophetically before the Lord. The way to do this is by surrendering your ear to the Holy Spirit and just allowing Him to play through you. The power playing music to set the mood can be seen even in the market place where certain genres of music are played at the spa or certain offices depending on whatever atmosphere one is trying to create. So now imagine this being done excellently in the sanctuary before the service starts. You have gone ahead and created the theme of what you will be singing that day and released it into the atmosphere. It is also good for the minstrels and the psalmists to come together and just sing to the Lord, not just for service. This is very powerful and creates a King David type of worship where he had psalmists and minstrels singing before the Lord twenty four seven. It is in this environment that new songs are created. Especially if you are singing the word to the Lord, you will notice that spontaneous song easily flows out of you. Every time you start testifying about Jesus and lifting Him up, He dominates the atmosphere. He goes where He is invited, exalted and enthroned.

Intercessory prayer

This is another way to shift the atmosphere. This is why in every worship team there must be intercessors specifically in the group for that only. You will now understand why I said previously that in my team I had some team members whose job was not to sing but to pray. Each person has to have a prayer life but these are only assigned prayer in the team for the church. The reason for this is because intercessory prayer requires a lot of fighting and exertion upon the intercessor and sometimes using the voice so hard can interfere with singing so it really helps when you have people in the team specifically for this. If you do not have intercessors in your team, you are the intercessor and let's not forget that sometimes the Lord will actually want *you the leader* to lead the prayer even though you have people assigned to this. Understand that prayer is like a plough. Do all the hard work before ministry so that when you come on the altar you have already made it easier for yourself in private preparation.

Fasting

This is where you go without food for a while and consecrate yourself in order to seek the Lord. It does not twist the arm of the Lord into doing stuff for you but it sensitizes you to the Spirit. This is one of the ways that the Lord releases supernatural power into your life. It shifts the atmosphere because there are some things that will not move just by a command. You have to add fasting to it to act like a backing power to your prayer. It sharpens your spiritual senses so that in your command of worship you are laser sharp and not just beating about the bush. It allows you to hit the bulls' eye in your command. Develop this into your worship and you will see what a difference it makes.

CHAPTER 10

The Price of worship

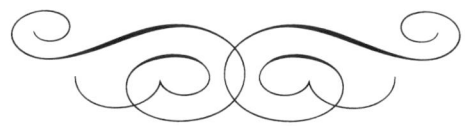

Let's bring up the Ark of the Lord

2 Samuel 6:1-23 says,

"Again, David gathered all the choice men of Israel, thirty thousand.
And David arose and went with all the people who were with him from
Baale Judah to bring up from there the ark of God, whose name is called by
the Name, the Lord of Hosts, who dwells between the cherubim. So they set
the ark of God on a new cart, and brought it out of the house of Abinadab,
which was on the hill; and Uzzah and Ahio, the sons of Abinadab, drove
the new cart. And they brought it out of the house of Abinadab, which
was on the hill, accompanying the ark of God; and Ahio went before the
ark. Then David and all the house of Israel played music before the Lord
on all kinds of instruments offir wood, on harps, on stringed instruments,

on tambourines, on sistrums, and on cymbals. And when they came to Nachon's threshing floor, Uzzah put out his hand to the ark of God and took hold of it, for the oxen stumbled. Then the anger of the Lord was aroused against Uzzah, and God struck him there for his error; and he died there by the ark of God. And David became angry because of the Lord's outbreak against Uzzah; and he called the name of the place Perez Uzzah to this day. David was afraid of the Lord that day; and he said, "How can the ark of the Lord come to me?" So David would not move the ark of the Lord with him into the City of David; but David took it aside into the house of Obed-Edom the Gittite. The ark of the Lord remained in the house of Obed-Edom the Gittite three months. And the Lord blessed Obed-Edom and all his household. Now it was told King David, saying, "The Lord has blessed the house of Obed-Edom and all that belongs to him, because of the ark of God." So David went and brought up the ark of God from the house of Obed-Edom to the City of David with gladness. And so it was, when those bearing the ark of the Lord had gone six paces, that he sacrificed oxen and fatted sheep. Then David danced before the Lord with all his might; and David was wearing a linen ephod. So David and all the house of Israel brought up the ark of the Lord with shouting and with the sound of the trumpet.

Now as the ark of the Lord came into the City of David, Michal, Saul's daughter, looked through a window and saw King David leaping and whirling before the Lord; and she despised him in her heart. So they brought the ark of the Lord, and set it in its place in the midst of the tabernacle that David had erected for it. Then David offered burnt offerings and peace offerings before the Lord. And when David had finished offering burnt offerings and peace offerings, he blessed the people in the name of the Lord of hosts. Then he distributed among all the people, among the whole multitude of Israel, both the women and the men, to everyone a loaf of bread, a piece of meat, and a cake of raisins. So all the people departed, everyone to his house.

Then David returned to bless his household. And Michal the daughter of Saul came out to meet David, and said, "How glorious was the king of Israel today, uncovering himself today in the eyes of the maids of his servants, as one of the base fellows shamelessly uncovers himself!"

So David said to Michal, "It was before the Lord, who chose me instead of your father and all his house, to appoint me ruler over the people of the Lord, over Israel. Therefore I will play music before the Lord. And I will be even more undignified than this, and will be humble in my own sight. But as for the maidservants of whom you have spoken, by them I will be held in honor."

Therefore Michal the daughter of Saul had no children to the day of her death.

When David was made king, he decided that he was going to bring the ark of the Lord back to its rightful place in and so he got a cart and two oxen to do the job. It sounded like an easy thing to just retrieve the ark of the Lord and get it back as quickly as possible. David was really hungry for the presence of the Lord and wanted the job done as quickly as possible but little did he know that there were very specific instructions that had been given to Moses on how to handle the ark of the Lord. He did not research or seek the Lord on how to do it. And in failing to do that, it resulted in the death of Uzzah. Now I would like to point out something important here. The Ark of the Covenant was in

Abinadab's house for twenty years and Uzzah had grown around it so to him it was just another box and it was common like any other box. It is just like our age where we do not reverence the Lord as we should. The bible says that David was afraid of the Lord that day and he went to every extent to learn what had been instructed to Moses about the ark. On his second attempt, he carefully followed the instructions given by appointing real men from the tribe of Levi to carry the ark from Obed Edom's house.

I want us to use this process of bringing the ark to Jerusalem as a symbol of bringing the manifested presence of the Lord in our midst. The Ark of the Covenant was a box of gopher wood overlaid with gold inside and out. It measured about four feet long, two and a half feet wide, and two and a half feet deep. It had a gold top with two solid gold cherubim on it. You can now see that this thing was heavy and the most logical thing would be to get an ox to carry it or in our modern day, a good ole' truck. But the Lord insisted that it be carried by the Levites. According to some theologians, the distance from Obededom's house to Jerusalem was about ten miles, and they had to carry the heavy ark on their shoulders. This doesn't make any sense at all that the Lord would want these men to carry such a heavy box on their shoulders for ten miles. Wasn't he mindful of how tired they would get considering the temperatures of that day? And to make the matters worse, David went above and beyond and wanted them to stop every six paces to make a sacrifice to the Lord. I don't think they were allowed to put the Ark of the Covenant down as the people sacrificed. The Lord was trying to make it clear that His presence does not come on the backs of dumb animals it comes when men and women understand the responsibility and feel the weight of His presence! So now, imagine how much longer the journey had become!

Imagine what a sweaty day that must have been for the Levites. Count six steps and then sacrifice an ox without putting the Ark of the Covenant down to catch some breath! This is just to show us how it's supposed to be. For the glory of God to come down in our life, city, church etc. someone has to get to work. I am not referring to works unto salvation here but the cost of true worship is unseen! These guys paid a dear price to usher the Ark of the Covenant into their city that day. The cart in this scenario represents the short cut or easy way out but this will not be the case. For us to see revival in our lives and for it to trickle down to the church and cities, we have to pay the price. Someone has to be the wood for the fire to burn. Someone has to live a sacrificial life of consecration before the Lord. Someone has to deny themselves of the normal things in life.

The truth is, when it comes to the real work, most of us do not want to work and we prefer to bask in what someone else has labored for. We would rather wait in line for hours to be anointed by someone instead of getting the real oil from the presence of the Lord. We will not study the word of God for ourselves; we want someone else to labor and then deliver it to us on a silver platter on Sunday morning and God help them if they do not work us into a frenzy. We want to feel high when we leave the service. This explains why we are more of spectators in worship instead of participators and our services are more people friendly than God- friendly. And you hear statements like *"I want your anointing"* implying that if we *touch or get hands laid on us* by someone else that their anointing that they have labored for so much in private, will come upon us and all we have to do is now function in it. This is the biggest lie ever told! God is not mocked, and whatever we sow is what we will reap. Unless it is an instruction from the Lord for this to be done on someone who is already laboring in private and He wants to establish something in their lives, why would the Lord allow for such an injustice? Injustice because it is not fair to the person that led a completely sacrificial life and then for a lazy person to come in and get it all by using their sweat rag. The devil is a liar! Go and work for your own anointing! The wonderful song by Cece Winans *you don't know the cost of the oil in my alabaster box* just comes to mind when I think about this.

Can you imagine how worn out the Levites must have been after that ten mile walk with the Ark of the Covenant on their shoulders in the hot sun? What if it was raining? The bible does not let us know the weather conditions of that day so let's use our imagination. All the other people did was enjoy that the Ark of the Covenant had been brought into Jerusalem and they screamed and danced alongside but what they did not understand was the price that had been paid for that to happen. You can even see how much they didn't understand the price that had been paid for this to happen in how Michal, David's wife speaks to him about all that dancing that he was doing before the ark of the covenant. She was offended by what she could not understand and therefore ended up being barren for the rest of her life.

How many times have you scorned people in your heart because you thought that their worship was too extravagant and you just felt that they were doing too much and surely, it didn't take all that to worship! Could this be the cause of the barrenness in a certain area of your life? The bible seems to insinuate that because Michal scorned the king on this day, he did not get intimate with her ever again thus the barrenness. 2 Samuel 6:20-23(Amp) *then David returned to bless his household. But (his wife) Michal the daughter of Saul came out to meet David and said, "How glorious and distinguished was the king of Israel today, who uncovered himself and stripped (off his kingly robes) in the eyes of his servants' maids like one of the riffraff who shamelessly uncovers himself!" So David said to Michal, "It was before the Lord (that I did this), who chose me above your father and all hishouse to appoint me as ruler over Israel, the people of the Lord. Therefore I will celebrate (in pure enjoyment) before the Lord. Yet I will demean myself even more than this, and will be humbled (abased) in my own sight (and yours, as I please), but by the maids whom you mentioned, by them I shall be held in honor." Michal the daughter of Saul had no children to the day of her death.*

So then it comes as no surprise that later in his life David would never offer the Lord sacrifices that cost him nothing because that day when he tried to use a shortcut to transport the Ark of the Covenant, he learnt something about the Lord. We are not to be *transporters* of the glory but *carriers* of the glory! 2 Samuel 24:18-25 *and Gad came that day to David and said to him, "Go up, erect an altar to the Lord on the threshing floor of Araunah the Jebusite." So David, according to the word of Gad, went up as the Lord commanded. 20 Now Araunah looked, and saw the king and his servants coming toward him. So Araunah went out and bowed before the king with his face to the ground.*

Then Araunah said, "Why has my lord the king come to his servant?" And David said, "To buy the threshing floor from you, to build an altar to the Lord, that the plague may be withdrawn from the people." Now Araunah said to David, "Let my lord the king take and offer up whatever seems good to him. Look, here are oxen for burnt sacrifice, and threshing implements and the yokes of the oxen for wood. All these, O king, Araunah has given to the king."

And Araunah said to the king, "May the Lord your God accept you."

Then the king said to Araunah, "No, but I will surely buy it from you for a price; nor will I offer burnt offerings to the Lord my God with that which costs me nothing." So David bought the threshing floor and the oxen for fifty shekels of silver. And David built there an altar to the Lord, and offered burnt offerings and peace offerings. So the Lord heeded the prayers for the land, and the plague was withdrawn from Israel.

I think that David learned the same vital lesson that we are learning here today when he was trying to get the Ark of the Covenant back to Jerusalem. That someone has to pay the price to carry the glory of God back into our churches, cities and lives. It is evident in the past revivals that we have read about in previous years. How certain people put their lives on the line to pray for revival until it showed up. What we offer unto the Lord must be ***the special offering*** not just what we can get by with, not that we are to be full of works since the main sacrifice was already given on Calvary but offering ourselves continually not just when it suits us. This includes our money, time etc. – every aspect of our lives.

We see that after he now prepared a tabernacle for the Ark of the Covenant that he followed the proper order as commanded by the Lord and appointed the Levites to handle it.

2 Chronicles 15:1-13 *David built houses for himself in the City of David; and he prepared a place for the ark of God, and pitched a tent for it. Then David said, "No one may carry the ark of God but the Levites, for the Lord has chosen them to carry the ark of God and to minister before Him forever." And David gathered all Israel together at Jerusalem, to bring up the ark of the Lord to its place, which he had prepared for it. Then David assembled the children of Aaron and the Levites: of the sons of Kohath, Uriel the chief, and one hundred and twenty of his brethren; of the sons of Merari, Asaiah the chief, and two hundred and twenty of his brethren; of the sons of Gershom, Joel the chief, and one hundred and thirty of his brethren; of the sons of Elizaphan, Shemaiah the chief, and two hundred of his brethren; of the sons of Hebron, Eliel the chief, and eighty of his brethren; of the sons of Uzziel, Amminadab the chief, and one hundred and twelve of his brethren .And David called for Zadok and Abiathar the priests, and for the Levites: for Uriel, Asaiah, Joel, Shemaiah, Eliel, and Amminadab. He said to them, "You are the heads of the fathers' houses of the Levites; sanctify yourselves, you and your brethren, that you may bring up the ark of the Lord God of Israel to the place I have prepared for it. For because you did not do it the first time, the Lord our God broke out against us, because we did not consult Him about the proper order."*

Before we leave these two scriptures on the transporting of the Ark of the Covenant there is a person I'd like us to look at; Obed Edom. He is first introduced to us in the Bible just after the death of Uzzah who was struck by the Lord for touching the Ark of the Covenant during the King David's first attempt to move it to Jerusalem. The Ark of the Covenant was placed in his home. I can imagine the terror that came with this because someone had just been killed by the roadside for mishandling the Ark yet he did not refuse to host it. It remained in his house for three months and the bible says that the Lord blessed his household and everything he owned. This must have been because he probably also did his research on how to handle the Ark of the Covenant and he taught it to his entire household. Three months went by and it was time for the ark to be moved to Jerusalem. He had a choice. He could have stayed where he was and live off of what he enjoyed with the Lord for those three months but he followed the Ark of the Covenant to Jerusalem.

He ended up becoming a gatekeeper, musician and a doorkeeper for the Ark of the Covenant but it did not end there. He kept going higher in God. He did such a good job taking care of the Ark in his house such that he was appointed to do it in Jerusalem. He became one of the worship leaders and is mentioned along with Asaph the chief musician. He ministered regularly before the Lord in worship as he still keeps the gates. His children were also serving alongside their father. He and his entire household were sixty eight brethren in total all serving in the house of the Lord. He paid a big price because he had to move his entire family and follow the Ark of the Covenant. He had enjoyed such intimacy with the Lord for those three months and had made up his mind that wanted to be where God was. No price was too high for him to pay to be where the presence of God was. It is not written anywhere that King David asked him to leave his home so we know that he did it out of his own free will. I'm sure a lot of people in his village must have criticized him and probably said the Ark killed one and has now made one crazy because of his radical decision to follow it but Obed Edom did not care. He and his family are the only ones who knew what went on with the Ark behind closed doors. His desire for the presence of God created an inheritance not only for himself but his entire household. And here we are today talking about him. This kind of thirst is not just birthed overnight; I really believe this man must have been seeking the Lord and it just so happened that there was a bump on the road near where he lived and Uzzah had to stretch out his hands and get struck and there was no other place to take the ark of the covenant other than Obed Edom's house. Selah

Part of the lifestyle that has been required of me is that of separation. I embrace and understand it now that I know my purpose in life. You see, there is the calling on your life and then there is the lifestyle that comes with it. A lot of people get the calling part right but forget to inquire from the Lord the type of lifestyle that is required of them to make sure they fulfill their calling. This is what Manoah was asking the angel of the Lord when they were told about the birth of Samson. He pleaded with the Lord to let the angel of the Lord *come back and teach them what they shall do for the child who will be born* and the instruction that had been given was that Samson *have no wine or similar drink nor would he eat anything unclean and that he would be a Nazirite to God from the womb until the day of his death.* That was the lifestyle required of him so that he would fulfil the purpose for which he was sent. Every time one's lifestyle is not in congruence with the assignment they have been given, they never see the fullness of their purpose.

Judges 13:1-13 Again *the children of Israel did evil in the sight of the Lord, and the Lord delivered them into the hand of the Philistines for forty years. Now there was a certain man from Zorah, of the family of the Danites, whose name was Manoah; and his wife was barren and had no children. And the Angel of the Lord appeared to the woman and said* to her, "Indeed now, you are barren and have borne no children, but you shall conceive and bear a son. Now therefore, please be careful not to drink wine or similar drink, and not to eat anything unclean. For behold, you shall conceive and bear a son. And no razor shall come upon his head, for the child shall be a Nazirite to God from the womb; and he shall begin to deliver Israel out of the hand of the Philistines."

So the woman came and told her husband, saying, "A Man of God came to me, and His countenance as like the countenance of the Angel of God, very awesome; but I did not ask Him where He was from, and He did not tell me His name. And He said to me, 'Behold, you shall conceive and bear a son. Now drink no wine or similar drink, nor eat anything unclean, for the child shall be a Nazirite to God from the womb to the day of his death.' " Then Manoah prayed to the Lord, and said, "O my Lord, please let the Man of God whom You sent come to us again and teach us what we shall do for the child who will be born."

And God listened to the voice of Manoah, and the Angel of God came to the woman again as she was sitting in the field; but Manoah her husband was not with her. Then the woman ran in haste and told her husband, and said to him, "Look, the Man who came to me the other day has just now appeared to me! "So Manoah arose and followed his wife. When he came to the Man, he said to Him, "Are You the Man who spoke to this woman?"

And He said, "I am." Manoah said, "Now let Your words come to pass! What will be the boy's rule of life, and his work? "So the Angel of the Lord said to Manoah, "Of all that I said to the woman let her be careful. She may not eat anything that comes from the vine, nor may she drink *wine or similar drink, nor eat anything unclean. All that I commanded her let her observe."*

Although some people might think that I am odd because I love spending a lot of time by myself seeking the Lord and I *choose* not to get into most activities. I love this about me and I center my life on the Lord and just minister to Him. I have always been like this but now I understand it more as I move deeper into my purpose. I remember several occasions when one of my friends who has now gone to be with the Lord would insist that we go dancing in town. I was still in Kenya then. She loved reggae and wanted me to join her in having a good time. I agreed to go with her one time but around the same time is when the Lord had started drawing me deeper into Him so I hid out in the restrooms and was just weeping and worshiping. It was finally time to go home and she found me after looking for me all over the building and after that night she had sworn to never take me anywhere because I had acted strange and embarrassed her. Overtime, I came to understand that this is the price I must pay for my calling. I miss out on a lot of parties not because I don't want to have a good time but it is part of the requirement of my calling, this is especially true because I lead worship at my local church and for those who know me, this is not a task I take lightly. I believe that every time I am leading worship there is a very specific task at hand for me that day and an even greater privilege is to be ministering to the Lord -the highest job ever! I prepare intensely in the presence of the Lord seeking from Him the direction He wants me to follow when I mount the altar. I minister to Him privately before I go on the altar as I ask the Holy Spirit to help me be in sync with the His agenda for that day. As I said earlier, my desire is to saturate Him so much and pour my love on Him until He has no other option than to move and I get so much fulfillment when I am ministering to Him and I see His reaction to my worship! So, rather than be at a party on Saturday night with my peers, I'd rather quiet myself in the presence of the Lord as I minister to Him. There are times when I've had to go to an event on Saturday night but this is only in times when I am not leading worship the next morning. I feel that when I do this it takes away from the preparation and focus.

There have been times when I tried to fit in by not being so weird but I would always pop out of what I was trying to get myself into because I didn't belong there! An extraordinary call demands an extraordinary consecration and results are determined by your obedience to the lifestyle that Lord is demanding of you. Your private devotion to the Lord matters a lot and when you make up your mind to honor the Lord in your lifestyle, He will honor you by showing up everywhere you go. It is like when a father has been practicing playing a certain game with his child and then the day that this child has to play in front of hundreds he shows up to cheer her on. This is the same way our heavenly Father is.

Keeping the fire

If you want the glory of God to be manifested in your church or city, **be the wood that keeps the flame** going. Feed the fire, and whatever you do, don't let the fire go out. The fire on the altar has to continue burning. We are always praying for the Lord to add fire to our fire in order to keep it burning, but this is not the case. Even in the natural, if you want fire to keep burning, all you have to do is to give it something to consume.

As long as there is something to consume, the fire will keep going. The only time fire dies is when there is nothing to feed it. So, if you feel that the fire within you is dwindling away, you don't have to ask the Lord for more fire upon the little fire within you, ask yourself, *"what am I feeding the fire?"* For the fire to burn there has to be wood constantly put into the fire to make sure it doesn't go out. Are you willing to be the wood for the fire in your life, city and region to burn or are you just going to be one of the spectators who sit around the bonfire to enjoy it completely oblivious to what is needed to keep it burning? One person cannot do this by themselves; we have to be willing to do our part.

Leviticus 6:9-13

"Command Aaron and his sons, saying, 'This is the law of the burnt offering: The burnt offering shall be on the hearth upon the altar all night until morning, and the fire of the altar shall be kept burning on it. And the priest shall put on his linen garment, and his linen trousers he shall put on his body, and take up the ashes of the burnt offering which the fire has consumed on the altar, and he shall put them beside the altar. Then he shall take off his garments, put on other garments, and carry the ashes outside the camp to a clean place. And the fire on the altar shall be kept burning on it; it shall not be put out. And the priest shall burn wood on it every morning, and lay the burnt offering in order on it; and he shall burn on it the fat of the peace offerings. A fire shall always be burning on the altar; it shall never go out.

The statement about making sure that the fire doesn't go out is repeated over and over in this scripture. And I will repeat this to you today, the only way a fire dies is when you don't feed it. The fire goes out when you stop offering yourself to God continually. Fire does not revive fire. The parts of your life that need to be consumed in the presence of the Lord are what revive the fire. When the Lord says *"I want this part of your life"* give it to Him and when you throw it into the fire, that's what keeps the fire going! Hebrews 12:29 says, *"for our God is a consuming fire."* Every time you withhold something from God that He is asking you to lay down, it causes the fire to go out. You are the keeper of your flame. It is your responsibility to keep your fire burning; you maintain it by continuous surrender to the Lord. What are you feeding your fire?

Another way to feed your fire is through **studying the word of God** and we have seen in previous chapters how this fans the flame within us. It also gives you the vocabulary you need while worshiping the Lord. You don't have to go to social media to get quotes to try and figure out what to tell Him. He has given you all you need in His word. Speak it back to Him. Many of us are walking around with malnourished spirits because we never feed our spirit man. Our natural body gets three meals a day and several snacks in between meals (and you have to understand that some of these snacks are meals too). So when you get in a battle with your flesh, don't be surprised when your flesh wins because it's stronger than your spirit man. Feed your spirit the word of God! 2 Timothy 2:15 says *"study to show thyself approved unto God, a workman that needeth not to be ashamed, rightly dividing the word of truth."* The only person you're supposed to be proving yourself to is the Lord. Don't do it for men or so that you can have a word to hit someone upside the head with when you get into an argument. Do it to for the Lord to feed your fire.

Fasting is also another way to feed your fire. Through the battering ram of prayer and fasting, you will be able to enforce the authority given to you as you open your mouth to worship.

CHAPTER II

The Higher Call

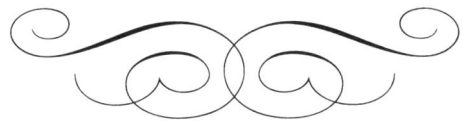

1 chronicles 27:28

And over the olive trees and the sycomore trees that were in the low plains was Baalhanan the Gederite: and over the cellars of oil was Joash:

In the above scripture we see how David appointed officials to serve in the kingdom. He placed each one of them where they were but I want us to focus specifically on Joash who was over the king's oil. There many interpretations of this scripture but I want us to focus mainly on keeping the oil. Oil here represents the Holy Spirit and Joash's duty was to make sure that the king's oil was protected. Even though his job was in a cellar away from the glory of the palace, he was faithful at it. As worshipers, we are to keep the oil that has been poured upon us by the King faithfully. The enemy of our souls is busy trying to get to this treasure that has been given to us by the Lord and he will use anything or anyone to accomplish that.

1 Timothy 6:20 *O Timothy! Keep what was committed to your trust,* Here we see Paul admonishing Timothy to guard what had been committed to him by the Lord. The word *keep* here means to guard (from loss or injury) properly by keeping the eye upon- implying that it could be lost, stolen or defiled by the enemy.

As a worshiper, it is your responsibility to protect what has been deposited in you by the Holy Spirit. What you carry within you is holy and you cannot take it everywhere or do everything that everyone is doing. It is like a pregnant mother who has to take such tender care of the life that is growing within her. You might not be pregnant with a baby right now but you are pregnant with the glory of God within you. Not participating in most activities does not mean that you are better than other people; it just means that you have chosen to be picky like a pregnant woman because you know what you are carrying.

This is why it is so important for you to inquire from the Lord the type of lifestyle you ought to live as it pertains to your calling. Just like Manoah and his wife inquired of the Lord about the rule of life (purpose) of the son that was to be born so that they would know how to raise Samson. In their case, the angel of the Lord even went into the details of what the child should do and what he shouldn't do in the course of his life. He would deliver Israel from the Philistines. Not only was he to let his hair grow long and to abstain from wine, strong drink and unclean food from birth to death, his mother was also commanded to remain pure so that even from the womb the child would be consecrated to the Lord. And they raised him that way- until Samson as an adult, started making his own decisions, because although the angel told his parents about his lifestyle, that decision had to ultimately be decided by Samson when he grew up.

No wine or liquor was to touch Samson's lips, his hair which was a sign of consecration as a Nazirite was not to be shaved. Nazirites today may not bear this outward mark of long hair but they are to be totally set apart for the Lord's holy purposes.

A high standard of purity that is being demanded for carriers of the glory of God is one that chooses to abstain from what is acceptable to society for the purpose of gaining the unobtainable. For example the many forms of entertainment, books, television, movies that fill our minds and spirits with filth and thus contaminate the deposit of the Holy Spirit within us.

The story of Samson is told in the book of Judges Chapters 13 through 16. It tells us of a man marked by God even before he was born yet whose story ends very tragically because he did not guard what was committed to his trust. A man who had such a great destiny and supernatural strength!

In Judges 16:17 the Bible says *"that he told her all his heart and said to her, "No razor has ever come upon my head, for I have been a Nazirite unto God from my mother's womb. If I am shaven, then my strength will leave me, and I shall become weak and be like any other man"* The enemy's only interest in Samson was to disgrace him and this is the still his agenda in your life- to find out where your strength comes from and then strip you of it and make you common because he is jealous that the Lord has set you apart for His work with His holy oil.

The Nazirite vow is found in Numbers 6:1-9 says, " *Then the Lord spoke to Moses, saying, "Speak to the children of Israel, and say to them: 'When either a man or woman consecrates an offering to take the vow of a Nazirite, to separate himself to the Lord, he shall separate himself from wine and similar drink; he shall drink neither vinegar made from wine nor vinegar made from similar drink; neither shall he drink any grape juice, nor eat fresh grapes or raisins. All the days of his separation he shall eat nothing that is produced by the grapevine, from seed to skin."*

'All the days of the vow of his separation no razor shall come upon his head; until the days are fulfilled for which he separated himself to the Lord, he shall be holy. Then he shall let the locks of the hair of his head grow. All the days that he separates himself to the Lord he shall not go near a dead body. He shall not make himself unclean even for his father or his mother, for his brother or his sister, when they die, because his separation to God is on his head. All the days of his separation he shall be holy to the Lord.

'And if anyone dies very suddenly beside him, and he defiles his conse-crated head, then he shall shave his head on the day of his cleansing; on the seventh day he shall shave it.

The word Nazirite comes for the root word *Nazir* which **means set apart for God, sanctified, and consecrated to reflect God's glory. It also means to remove from common standard in order to meet the standard of God.** This is what Samson had been called into.

The saddest verse in the bible according to me is found in Judges 16:20 The Bible says "And *she said, "The philistines are upon you, Samson!" so he awoke from his sleep, and said, "I will go out as before, at other times, and shake myself free!" BUT HE DID NOT KNOW THAT THE LORD HAD DEPARTED FROM HIM."* (Emphasis mine) this is what happens when we do not guard what was committed to our trust and we continue with life as usual not knowing that the presence of Lord has departed from us. As a worshiper, you have been entrusted with a very high calling. To host the presence of the Lord and it is not something you can just take lightly. Take yourself seriously and recognize the high office you have been placed in by the Lord. That when you lift your voice, He shows up! We are to be distinguished not by anything else but the presence of the Lord. Distance yourself from anything that could defile this call on your life by becoming so God centered such that nothing else matters.

2 Corinthians 6:17 says, " *Therefore, "come out from among them and be separate, says the Lord. Do not touch what is unclean, and I will receive you."* The separation that Paul is talking about here is not the separation from contact with the world because we can't help this as we are here currently, but it is the ***separation from complacency and conforming to the patterns of this world.*** We are to separate ourselves from anything that would cause us to honor Him with our lips but keep Him at bay in our hearts.

Others can but I cannot! Not because I am better than them, but because of what I am carrying within me. Always remember this each time you are confronted with a decision to choose something that feels okay to everyone else but *doesn't sit right with your spirit.* We see this also in Daniel 1:8 the Bible says, "*But Daniel purposed in his heart that he would not defile himself with the portion of the king's delicacies, nor with the wine which he drank; therefore he requested of the chief of the eunuchs that he might not defile himself.*" There was nothing wrong with the king's food but Daniel knew his call and knew that if he partook of it, it would defile him so he chose not to. He understood that others could, but *he* could not. By doing this, he and his friends were highly distinguished from the other wise men in their time. As you separate yourself, know that it is not in vain. The Lord sees your sacrifice and will reward you accordingly.

A higher call in God demands complete separation as we see in Acts 13:2 *As they ministered to the Lord and fasted, the Holy Spirit said, "Now separate to Me Barnabas and Saul for the work to which I have called them.* "The Holy Spirit demanded this of Barnabas and Saul and it is my strong belief that had they not separated themselves to the Lord, they would not have seen the fullness of their destiny. What God has separated, let no man commonize!

Dear reader, there is a strong oil on your life for worship and Beelzebub the lord of the flies is jealous about it. He is working overtime trying to find a way to contaminate your oil. He does this by studying and then keying in on your weaknesses. Close every door to him and light your life on fire for God. Flies like to rest on oil and thus contaminate it and what attracts them is the garbage we allow in our lives. Clean up your house from the inside out and live a life poured out before the Lord. You carry a great treasure within you so protect the oil of worship at all costs!

If you want to soar in your worship, you must separate yourself and have a single eyed devotion to the Lord. Set yourself apart to be used of God. May the Lord draw you nearer to Him through His Holy Spirit as you recommit your life to Him as a carrier of His presence. Amen